Five Ways to Color Your Retirement GREEN

WHAT YOU NEED TO KNOW SO YOU WON'T RUN
OUT OF MONEY JUST WHEN YOU NEED IT MOST

Jack Teboda

Teboda & Associates
ELGIN, ILLINOIS

Jack Teboda/Teboda & Associates
81 Market Street, Suite 5
Elgin, IL 60123
www.teboda.com

Book layout ©2013 BookDesignTemplates.com

Ordering Information:
Quantity sales. Special discounts are available on quantity purchases by corporations, associations and others. For details, contact the address above.

Five Ways to Color Your Retirement GREEN/ Jack Teboda. —1st ed.
ISBN-13: 978-1522871132

Contents

I dedicate this book to my beautiful wife of more than 40 years, Babs. Over the years, I was able to concentrate on my career knowing she was managing the home front and nurturing our children into the fine people they are today.

I know I would not be the man I am today without her dedication, love and support. Thank you for being you.

Preface

I am an optimist by nature. To me, the glass is always half full, not half empty. I see the good in my fellow man. I see the potential of our society to achieve and soar to new heights of accomplishment.

I am also a realist. I see things for what they are, not through rose-colored glasses. Just because I focus on the good doesn't mean I do not see the bad for what it is. The difference is I try to see a way forward to make it better. I think it is this philosophical bent more than anything else that led me down the career path of that of a problem-solver.

Once there were three men named Optimist, Pessimist and Realist. They were all aboard a ship at sea when suddenly an explosion occurred, and the ship started to go up in flames. Each man's response to the situation was entirely different.

Optimist was so confident that all would work out just fine that he calmly went about his business as if nothing were wrong.

Pessimist was certain the ship was sinking. He yelled, "Abandon ship," and dove overboard into the icy sea.

Realist put on a life jacket and grabbed two more, one for each of his friends, Optimist and Pessimist, and then hurried to the nearest lifeboat and called out to them, urging them to jump into the boat with him before he lowered it into the water. As things turned out, Optimist, because he was certain nothing bad would happen, waited too late and went down with the ship. Pessimist died from hypothermia within minutes after his leap into the water. Only Realist made it through the disaster.

I am convinced that to survive and prosper in this economic world with its ever-changing landscape, fraught with misinformation and uncertainty, you need to harness the ability to see things clearly for what they are, and maintain the positive mental attitude that you can alter the outcome by taking appropriate action. Essentially, that is the message of this book, as you will see if you continue reading. We will not only identify some of the most pressing challenges for those who are in or near retirement, but we will also present solutions to those challenges. If some of those solutions are new to you, I urge you to consider them with an open mind and hear me out on them. Some of the best solutions to financial planning challenges involve innovative thinking.

Three Kinds of People

Astronaut James Lovell is credited with coining the axiom, "There are people who *make things happen*, there are people who *watch things happen* and there are people who *wonder what happened*."

Lovell is best known as the commander of the Apollo 13 mission, which was supposed to be the third landing of men on the moon in April 1970. I was in my early 20s back then, but I was very interested in the space program. I was intrigued by these brave men who risked their lives to explore the unknown. When I heard the news that there had been an explosion in deep space, crippling the command module carrying Lovell, Jack Swigert and Fred Haise, it slowly began to dawn on me that these men might not make it home. According to all reports, Lovell and his crew remained calm and, under the direction of Mission Control, set about adapting to and overcoming each obstacle that stood between them and a safe return to Earth. They had lost cabin heat and most of their battery power. They had to use the lunar landing craft as a lifeboat. When it became clear they were running out of breathable air, the astronauts jury-rigged a carbon dioxide removal system out of cardboard and duct tape. On April 17, 1970, to the great relief of every American and many outside the United States who watched and listened as the drama unfolded, the intrepid trio made it back, safe and sound, to the big blue marble from whence they came.

Nothing I can think of better exemplifies the optimist/realist mindset. They knew how grim their predicament was, but they took an assessment of what tools they had at their disposal and set about making things work in their favor. They *made things happen.*

Economic Freefall

On Oct. 9, 2007, the Dow peaked at 14,164. By March, 2009, the Dow had dropped nearly 54 percent from its high, ending up at 6,547, sparking what has been dubbed "the Great Recession." It is called that because, as recessions go, it was deeper and lasted longer than any before.

There are certain statistical rules for what a recession is, and when one begins and ends. According to the National Bureau of Economic Research (NBER), the Great Recession began in December 2007 and ended 18 months later in June 2009. According to a study conducted by two former U.S. Census Bureau officials, incomes continued to slide after the recession was officially over. Between June of 2009 and June of 2011, the median household annual income, adjusted for inflation, fell 6.7 percent to $49,909. There were no headlines proclaiming an end to the recession. When the NBER pinpoints the end of a recession, it has to do so in retrospect after they collect the data and analyze the numbers. But in 2012, if you had told the millions of Americans who are still unemployed (12 million as of July 2012) that the recession was over, they may have argued the point with you. For them, it was still ongoing. As President Harry S. Truman said, "It's a recession when your neighbor loses his job; it's a depression when you lose your own."

"What Happened?"

I had a speaking engagement shortly after the Dow dropped 777 points in one day on Sept. 29, 2008. It was a retirement seminar, and my audience was a room full of people who appeared stunned and worried.

Many of them had just seen the Wall Street ticker take away a large chunk of their life savings in one day. Their question, in brief, was "what happened?" There was no point in discussing the nuances of estate tax law, which was to be my topic, so I opened it up for questions and took them one at a time.

"What I cannot figure out is how the people in Washington could let something like this happen," said one frustrated man.

I had no answer for that one. All I could do was share his frustration. But his attitude was typical of others in the room — "Don't we have people in place who are supposed to prevent this sort of thing from happening? Were they all asleep at the wheel?"

The realist in me sees their point. There was too little watchfulness in government. There was also too much greed in the private sector. The optimist in me, however, chooses to find a ray of sunshine in the gloom. We learn from our mistakes. Just like those astronauts aboard the crippled spacecraft, we look at what assets we have left, and we go about the task of making our way safe again. We take stock of what we have after a disaster like that and put it to work more intelligently this time. We have heard the snap of the bear trap and felt it nip at our toes. Hopefully, we won't get that close to it again.

Pulling Back the Curtain

My inspiration for writing *"Five Ways to Color Your Retirement GREEN"* did not come in the form of a sudden epiphany the way an apple fell on the head of, who was it, Sir Isaac Newton? In the last three decades I have spent as a financial professional, I have learned many things I feel need to be passed along. My first job was as a teacher. The urge to communicate instructively just comes out from time to time. After sitting down with a number of new clients following the stock market tumble of 2008 and helping them pick up the pieces of their financial lives, I came to the conclusion that sharing what I have learned is necessary, and that I needed to express it in a more public format. My intention is to pull back the curtain, turn on the spotlight and focus it on some common misconceptions that endanger people's fortunes. As you read further, you will see that I pull no punches at exposing outdated money management ideas and misinformation that I believe work at cross purposes to sound income planning. It is my opinion that we live in uncertain and volatile times when it comes to caring for and preserving our assets. Those who survive and thrive will be those who are watchful and cautious. Those who succeed will be those who do nothing out of impulse but make decisions from a tested and true base of knowledge and sound research.

I subscribe to the notion that knowledge is power, but only when it is put to use. America's economic landscape is ever changing. Strategies and techniques that worked 30, 20 or even 10 years ago may not always work now. Attaining and maintaining financial independence in retirement requires clear thinking, accurate information and a willingness on our part to change tactics when necessary in order to have the kind of financial future we want. It is my hope that, through the pages of this book, you can better equip yourself for retirement, and that your "golden years" will indeed be golden.

"*Five Ways to Color Your Retirement GREEN*" will be a distillate of information I have gleaned as a financial professional, and advice and wisdom I have collected from others during the last three decades. I will share them with you at the end of this book. For now, let's consider our financial landscape and look at it telescopically first, and then microscopically in some cases to determine our position and what our most appropriate and effective response should be.

CHAPTER 1

The Case for "Going Green"

Green is not only the color of money, but has also become the buzzword for healing the planet and giving deeper thought to our every action involving the use of our resources, natural and otherwise. "Going green" is a concept unique to our time. It was the baby boom generation — those born between 1946 and 1964 — that first began focusing on cleaning up our air and water and preserving the rainforests of the world. Their social awareness spawned something else, however, that the tie-dyed T-shirt generation could never have expected.

It has become fashionable these days for corporations and other large institutions to "go green," not necessarily because such a course demonstrates sensitivity to the environment, but because it is more profitable.

You know darn well that when the retail giant Wal-Mart Stores Inc. "goes green," it is because it enhances their profits and not because a bunch of tree huggers took over the boardroom. The megachain started by the legendary Sam Walton has a worldwide reputation for squeezing every penny until Abe Lincoln hollers.

I recently read where Wal-Mart ordered its suppliers to reduce the size of their packaging. When you open a new cereal box, do you notice there is always some space at the top of the bag? That's because the flakes, or oats, or whatever, settles during shipping and the smaller pieces gather at the bottom. That bothered Wal-Mart execs. How many inches were wasted in this cardboard box? One? Two? Multiply that by millions and multiply that by thousands of shelves and acres of floor space and we are talking about some serious money here.

One of Wal-Mart's top suppliers, General Mills, found a way to reduce the size of the boxes used to package Cheerios by letting the cereal settle on the production line instead of during shipping. The result was that 10 percent more cereal fits into the boxes, and the cost savings ripple all the way through the pipeline.

It doesn't stop there. Going green allowed Wal-Mart to save millions of dollars on everything from wine bottles to shoe boxes. Just the change in the size of the Cheerios boxes alone resulted in a reduction of approximately 200,000 pounds of cardboard a year for General Mills. That's the equivalent of more than 1,000 trees! But that's beside the point. Fitting more cereal into less space meant more cereal could be hauled by fewer trucks. This saved 25,000 gallons of fuel and reduced General Mills' annual carbon footprint by 220 metric tons. Yes, of course, all of this helps save the planet, but the real and immediate savings, for both the cereal people and Wal-Mart, was at the bank.

Going Green Paradigm Shift

The green movement, ecologically speaking, gets its impetus from the awareness that our natural resource are finite and that conserving them is sensible. Just 200 years ago, when the vast frontier of the North American continent was inhabited only by Native Americans, settlers gave little thought to how much of *anything* they consumed. There was just so much of it! Centuries later, their great-great-great-grandchildren are learning the ways of the Native Americans, on whose land they settled, not to be so careless with Mother Nature.

But conservation and preservation aren't limited to an ecological sense. When it comes to our retirement, many of those who are in what I call the "red zone" of retirement (five years on either side of their retirement date) are beginning to think like Benjamin Franklin: "A penny saved is a penny earned."

There may have been a time when you could invest your way to a wealthy retirement. In the 1990s, we could do no wrong. The stock market kept going up, and there was no end in sight. Any strategy worked. The only question was, "How much will our portfolio go up today?"

Then came a rude awakening when the dot-com bubble burst in 2000. That financial earthquake changed our thinking. It was what they called a paradigm shift — a change in the way we look at things. For the first time, many of us realized that conservation and preservation of our financial resources are critical to our being able to enjoy them in our retirement. Then came the market crash of 2008. It was like learning that, not only could your pet bite, it could attack and kill small children! It was a paradigm shift of 8.6 on the Richter scale! As they say in sports, it was a "real game changer." If we weren't convinced before that we could not always count on the stock market to continue soaring ever upward, we were then. The market had giveth, and now the market had taketh away.

According to one analysis of the 2010 Survey of Consumer Finances conducted by the Federal Reserve, the median balance in 401(k)s and individual retirement accounts, or IRAs, for folks nearing retirement is $120,000. Unless your expenses are extremely low and your lifestyle is Spartan, that won't be enough. If you were to turn $120,000 into a joint-and-survivor annuity (nothing fancy; just turn the cash into a guaranteed lifetime payout), it would only yield around $600 per month.

How many Americans pumped money into their retirement accounts for decades expecting a comfortable retirement only to learn their money was not safe? A lot. That is why the mood has shifted to one of "going green"…that is to say, conserving their nest egg by spending less, saving more and investing more carefully.

The Rewards of Thrift and Caution

The rewards of cutting back on spending are significant. Try this: Sit down with a calculator and your annual expense ledger, and figure up where you could save money. Keep it reasonable. Let's say $2,000 per year. What do you spend money on that you could do without? You may discover in just a few minutes where you are wasting that much money.

For my personal finances, I have a simple, inexpensive computer program that creates a pie chart that tells me how much I spent dining out, going to the movies, traveling for pleasure, etc. It may shock you to see how much you could save just by trimming those budgets a bit. Remember, this exercise will do you no good if you don't take those dollars and save them. Over the course of a year, $2,000 is less than $170 per month. If you save that much for 20 years, you would have saved $40,000. With the miracle of compounding, and assuming a reasonable rate of return in a conservative investment, your money would double from interest by the time you retired.

Come Up With Your Number

Yogi Berra is credited with the slogan, "If you don't know where you're going, be careful, you might not get there."

Knowing your number means knowing what you need to have in the way of income when you retire. Once you know that, you can save toward that goal. That is the cornerstone of retirement planning — knowing your number. I advocate making an appointment with a financial professional who is trained in, and who specializes in, retirement income planning. He or she can see things you probably cannot see. You can benefit from their experience of working with hundreds of others just like you. If you don't already have a clear vision of how much you will need to cover your expenses in retirement, they will help you get one, and then they can help you devise a strategy that will take you there.

Balance is key here, folks. You don't want to be overly optimistic and run the risk of missing your goals, but neither do you want to be too pessimistic and sacrifice more of your current lifestyle than is reasonable. If your savings program is punitive, you won't stick with it. Retirement is a long-term proposition.

You must manage your expectations and remain flexible. Hey, life happens! Things change! No one knows the future. But steaming toward retirement without a plan is like taking an ocean voyage without a compass and a chart. The best you can do is plot a course, put probability on your side, and stick to your plan as closely as possible.

CHAPTER 2

You May Be a Baby Boomer If

Beside the chronological identifiers of the baby boom generation mentioned earlier (born between 1946 and 1964), there are other ways to tell if you are part of this unique generation. You are probably a baby boomer if:

- You know what is meant by "Howdy Doody time."
- You ever put tin foil on rabbit ears.
- You ever removed ice from metal trays with levers.
- You ever heard the command, "duck and cover."
- Your doctor, lawyer and accountant are older than you are.
- Your 80-something mother thinks you are a computer genius, but your 20-something child rolls their eyes when you ask technology questions.
- You would "tweet" if anybody showed you how.
- The name "Mr. Green Jeans" means something to you.
- Your father ever changed a tube on the TV set.
- You remember where you were when President John F. Kennedy was assassinated.
- Pay phones were everywhere, and the home phone was not called a "land line" because what else could it be?

- You remember where you were when Neil Armstrong said, "That's one small step for man…"
- You considered your grandparents to be old when they were the same age you are now.

One characteristic of boomers is that they tend to think of themselves as a special generation, different from those that came before. Well, it's true. They forged their own music and rhetoric and imposed it upon the world. They are not through weaving their unique pattern through the fabric of society, as we will point out in more detail later in this book.

Why the tag, "baby boomer?" There was a clearly discernible bulge in the birth rate after World War II. The employment surge brought on by the war had shocked the nation out of the depression doldrums, and the returning soldiers came back to a country just beginning to reacquaint itself with prosperity. They found jobs and started families and began to participate in the great American dream.

As a group, baby boomers have had a significant impact on society. Their generation is associated with both a redefinition of the traditional values held by their parents, although, frankly, not all of that has made for positive results. Boomers also grew up in a time of privilege and affluence. As a generation, they are the most active, most physically fit generation ever to emerge on the world scene. They are better-educated than their parents. On average, they earn more money than their parents did, even when you take inflation into account.

Boomers live an average of 10 years longer than did their parents. This could be due to a healthier lifestyle, or more sophisticated medicines and better medical care, or a combination.

The world was a cornucopia to boomers. Theirs was the first generation to grow up during a time when the government subsidized everything from housing to education. These free rides became so much the norm that they became entitlements to the boom generation. It is no wonder so many of them became lost in the fog of idealism that pervaded the 1960s. They went about with the glassy-eyed optimism of the children they were, genuinely expecting the world to improve now that they were poised to take the helm. Looking back now, that wild optimism has faded, replaced by a somewhat confident realism. But there can be no doubt that this generation, merely by the sheer force of its numbers, created a shockwave that remolded society.

A Wake-Up Call for Boomers

In the 2016 Retirement Confidence Survey conducted by the Employee Benefit Research Institute (EBRI), researchers quizzed workers age 55 and older about their retirement savings. The results were like a wake-up call for baby boomers. Here's what the survey found:

- 74% have less than $100,000 in retirement savings
- 54% have saved less than $25,000
- 26% have saved less than $1,000

One of the most telling statistics of the EBRI survey was that 51 percent of the workers surveyed said they had never calculated how much monthly income they would need in retirement, let alone done formal retirement income planning. Despite this, when asked how they felt they were doing when it came to preparing for retirement, 63 percent of them said they were somewhat or very confident about having enough money for a comfortable retirement.

Score: "A" for optimism. "F" for reality perception.

In my early 30s, I was a teacher. I taught physical education and drivers ed. I discovered that there was a varying level of depth perception among teenagers learning how to drive. Some had it instinctually. Others had to learn it. Depth perception is as vital to driving safety as an altimeter is to a skydiver. Understanding the relationship between distance and speed to pedestrians and other cars is fundamental. Some youngsters had to learn the hard way to not trust uneducated senses. As a teacher, I found that one of my greatest challenges was to educate students on how much they did not know. That was often where the learning process began.

It is that way with people and their money sometimes. That unbridled sense of optimism that seems to have engendered itself to baby boomers has had both a positive and a negative effect on their financial lives. Because things have always worked out for them in their lives, there is often a disconnect between perception and reality when it comes to how much they will need for their retirement. In the EBRI survey, more than half of those 45 and older said they had never tried to calculate how much they need to save for retirement. Most had no clue as to how much they would need in the way of income.

Even more sobering is the statistic that slightly more than 50 percent of retirees surveyed found that, despite expectations to the contrary, their spending in retirement was either higher than or equal to their pre-retirement spending.

Longevity — A Blessing and a Curse

A major conundrum of retirement planning is estimating how long you will live. Longevity is a good thing. Outliving your resources and losing your independence and, along with it, your dignity and sense of self-direction, is not so good.

What is the average life expectancy of the baby boomers? The short answer is around 84. But it is a bit more complicated than that. Interestingly, every year you live extends your life expectancy a little further. The longer you live, the longer you are *likely* to live. For instance, in America the life expectancy at birth is just short of 80 years of age. But if you make it to 65, then life expectancy jumps up to 86.3. If you survive to age 75, life expectancy jumps to 86.7. Compare that to previous generations. In 1900, the average life expectancy in the United States was 47. In 1960, it was 69. In 2004, the average life expectancy was 80. Some have projected that millions will live to well over 100 years of age in the next century. All this is wonderful, if we are making financial plans for it.

Contingency Thinking

When I taught driver's education for the Elgin School District in Elgin, Illinois, one of my favorite themes was developing the skill of what I called "contingency driving." This is when you are consistently able to, without even thinking about it, project in your mind possible scenarios while driving, enabling you to take instant action to avoid an accident. A deer could dash out in front of you. A truckload of logs could come undone from a tractor trailer just ahead. The list goes on and on.

"Slamming on the brakes is not always the best action to take," I told my students. "Try to always have an escape route as a backup in case a dangerous road situation should present itself."

Any experienced driver can testify that not every driver is a safe driver. Some are speeders. Some are lane-drifters. Some are tailgaters. Some drink and drive. Nowadays, you also have texters to worry about. Your contingency route could be the median on a divided highway. It could be the shoulder of the road or even a parking lot. Having the mental acuity to resist jamming on the brakes when you can brake, in control, to an area away from danger could save your life.

So it is in retirement planning. What happens if your health fails? How will you meet those medical expenses? What happens if your spouse dies? What if you just run out of savings? Do you have an escape route? Do you have a contingency plan?

Some financial advisors allow for only 25 years of retirement. I disagree. I advocate locking in *a lifetime guaranteed income* that will ensure you never run out of money. Some financial plans contain no escape clauses for the unexpected. But I am of the mindset that we need to expect the best and plan for the worst.

The Times, They Are A-Changin'
"Come senators, congressmen
Please heed the call
Don't stand in the doorway
Don't block up the hall

For he that gets hurt
Will be he who has stalled
There's a battle outside
And it is ragin'.
It'll soon shake your windows
And rattle your walls
For the times they are a-changin'."
— Bob Dylan, 1961

You may be a baby boomer if you remember that, too. Times are indeed changing for retirees. The decade that began in 2010 holds far less economic promise than the decade of the 1990s, especially for the ill-prepared. A few years ago, retirement planners often referred to what they called the "three-legged stool of retirement" — Social Security, your personal savings and your traditional pension. Today, it appears that two legs of that stool are shaky, and one has fallen off completely.

Traditional pensions have gone the way of the Edsel. Large companies, even the ones formerly known for their generous employee benefits, just aren't providing pensions to employees anymore. Workers who have a traditional defined benefit plan should consider themselves fortunate. These programs guarantee a lifetime income to the retiree and sometimes to his/her spouse. They are on the wane nowadays, mainly because of how costly those plans became to the companies that sponsored them. The word "guarantee" was quite expensive.

Defined *benefit* pension plans are being replaced in large measure by defined *contribution* plans, such as 401(k) plans, an idea that came of age in the 1990s. These programs shift the burden of saving and investing from employers to employees. They provide lots of opportunity, but there is risk there. The investing options can be confusing, and market-based products aren't guaranteed. These plans allow employees to save a portion of their paychecks and, unless employees withdraw their money before age 59 ½ and incur the 10 percent federal early withdrawal tax, they don't have to pay income taxes on their savings until they start distributions in retirement. Some employers match what the employee saves, and some do not. There is less and less enthusiasm on the part of employers for matching — which a 2014 article by Bloomberg, "Your Wilting Retirement: Company 401(k) Plans Get Stingy," highlighted as it named several Fortune 500 companies that were quietly phasing out their employee matching.

These plans allow employees to make their own investment choices, often with scant guidance. Many American workers, unsophisticated in the ways of investing, saw their defined contribution plans lose as much as 40 percent of their value in the last two market downturns. This served to further retard the accumulation of money these employees would need later on when they retired. The tragedy with some was that all their eggs were in that basket. Aside from their 401(k) or 403(b) at work, they had no other retirement savings.

Social Security — There is widespread skepticism regarding the long-term viability of Social Security. Why? Because the number of those receiving money from the Social Security system is increasing while the number of those paying into it decreases. It is no wonder that some perceive Social Security to be on the ropes and gasping for breath. The system is projected to run into a sticky situation by 2038 where there will be less coming into the system than there is going out, according to the 2014 OASDI Trustees Report. If Congress doesn't act to reform the system before that point, future benefits will have to be reduced. That leaves most boomers in the safe zone, but their children and grandchildren may not be so lucky. Many reform measures have been suggested to keep the ship afloat — everything from raising the retirement age and payroll taxes to revising the benefit formulae in a number of ways. There is even talk in some circles of privatizing Social Security and Medicare. All that notwithstanding, concern about the future of these government programs continues. What our parents regarded as good as gold and guaranteed is no longer that.

Baby boomers can be especially caught in a pickle here. Their parents could rely on pensions and Social Security for the bulk of their retirement income. The children of boomers are going in with no illusions. They know not to rely on either of the above. They have time to adjust and compensate. Boomers are caught in the middle, and the shifting of realities when it comes to retirement seems to have caught a number of them by surprise.

Where's the Big Wealth Transfer?

What about the trillions of dollars that was supposed to transfer from one generation to the other? I remember hearing a great deal about it in the news in the 1990s.

"Retirees constitute one of the wealthiest segments of the U.S. population," read one editorial, "with more personal wealth than any previous generation."[1]

Naturally, it was thought that this wealth would be bequeathed to baby boomers, thus serving to bridge the gap between their retirement needs and their assets. So far, I haven't seen this happening. Have you?

Apparently, aside from an old piano and maybe some photo albums, only around 20 percent of Americans ever receive an inheritance of any kind. For those who did receive an inheritance, the median inheritance was $73,000.[2] While no one would turn that down, it is a far cry from the millions implied by previous predictions. So, baby boomers, if you are unprepared for retirement and you were expecting a windfall from the previous generation, there goes some of the red off your candy. For some folks, the best you can hope for is that your parents will have enough to support themselves during their own retirement, and you won't become part of the new "sandwich generation." Those are the folks who are caring for dependent kids *and* dependent parents.

---

[1] Insurance Journal West Magazine. Feb. 23, 2004. "Baby Boomer Wealth Transfer." http://www.insurancejournal.com/magazines/features/2004/02/23/37126.htm

[2] Edward N. Wolff, Maury B. Gittleman. 2014. The Journal of Economic Inequality. "Inheritances and the distribution of wealth or whatever happened to the great inheritance boom?" 12.4 (2014): 439-468.

CHAPTER 3

Stop Overpaying Your Taxes

The scratchy sound of President Franklin Roosevelt's voice has been preserved from his first inaugural address in 1933. The country was in the grip of The Great Depression. Roosevelt, usually buoyant and charming, was unusually somber as he intoned to a pained public, "The only thing we have to fear is fear itself." The entire speech is a moving and hopeful treatise given by a paternal president soothing a hurting national family.

Abraham Lincoln was another great. I have read he did not trust his speeches to others and worked tirelessly on his prose. Who could forget the Gettysburg Address, where he proved that brevity of expression trumps long-windedness every time?

And of course, Ronald Reagan wasn't called the "great communicator" for nothing. Perhaps it was the thespian in him, but who else could have pulled off the one-liners like he did.

"Tear... down... this... wall!" he challenged the Soviet Premier Mikhail Gorbachev at the Berlin Wall's Brandenburg Gate in 1987. The wall did come down a few years later with the unraveling of the Soviet Union. When I saw the news video of cheering crowds with sledgehammers chipping away at the iconic symbol of Communist oppression, I could not help but think of how far things had come since John F. Kennedy intoned the words of the 1963 "Ich bin ein Berliner" speech near the same wall shortly after its construction.

Nine Terrifying Words

When it comes to witticisms that strike right to the heart of big government and poke fun at its tendencies to pick your pocket in the name of public service, perhaps no president compares to Reagan, who is credited with saying, "The nine most terrifying words in the English language are: *I'm from the government, and I'm here to help.*"

What was the former president talking about? Taxes, mostly. His conservative legacy was built on reining in big government, which he considered the stealthiest and greediest of all pickpockets. Reagan's Economic Recovery Tax Act (ERTA) is a timeless example of easing taxes to stimulate the economy. Bill Brown, a visiting professor of the practice of law at Duke University, said in a USA Today article in April 2009, "During the early days of the Reagan Administration, a time plagued by slow economic growth, high interest rates and runaway inflation, ERTA not only reduced tax rates, but established a powerful set of incentives to promote investment in income-producing 'capital assets' — plant, property and equipment." Brown credits ERTA and its 25 percent tax cuts for turning the country around from the economic woes that characterized the administration of President Jimmy Carter. Opponents of the measures would label it a giveaway to the rich since the tax burden of the wealthy would lower disproportionately with the tide. That's when we first started hearing the phrase "trickle-down economics." However, according to Brown, Reagan actually raised the tax burden for the wealthy. Individuals earning more than $200,000 per year, for instance, saw their taxes double from 7 percent in 1981 to 14 percent in 1986.

Paying Your Fair Share

No one likes to pay more than his or her fair share of anything. How would it be if the city where you live just divided up the total cost of the electricity used in your area by the number of homes, and sent each customer the same bill each month? That would be unfair to the conservative user who doesn't run the air conditioner for fear of wasting electricity. Or the little old lady on a fixed income who miserly turns out all the lights in unoccupied rooms. The poor sap who tries to conserve would be forced to subsidize the wastefulness of his careless neighbor.

Or what about the huge factory down the street that gobbles up millions of kilowatt hours to your measly 1,000 or so? How unfair it would be if you were forced to pay for their power bill.

When it comes to taxes, Americans send some $945 million too much to the Internal Revenue Service each year, according to a report issued by CBS News.

The overpayments are largely because of the Internal Revenue Service Code, which is a complex volume containing 7,500 pages and more than 3 million words. It seems obvious to me that those who pay more taxes than they should are those who are unfamiliar with the legal loopholes and tax breaks.

Ray Martin, a financial commentator on "The Early Show" on CBS, says the overpayments are largely because taxpayers don't take advantage of ordinary deductions to which they are entitled. He quotes a report issued by the federal Government Accountability Office, saying the number of tax returns on which itemized deductions are left off could be as high as 2.2 million.

The Death Tax

One of the most egregious examples of unfair taxation, however, is the federal estate tax, also known as the "death tax." Can you imagine telling your young children, "Don't save. Spend every dime you can. Do your level best to die penniless"?

And yet, that is the message this tax sends to the American people.

"Go ahead. Work hard, be thrifty and accumulate a fortune. You just will pass a lot of it on to Uncle Sam and not your heirs."

The estate tax has an interesting history. Taxation of property transfers at death can be traced all the way back to ancient Egypt as early as 700 B.C. Nearly 2,000 years ago, Roman Emperor Caesar Augustus imposed the "vicesima hereditatium," which was a tax on property left to heirs. In the middle ages, it was a custom in feudal Europe to make a family pay a year's rent, which amounted to a tax, when they inherited land. The term "stamp tax" or "death tax" was used to describe fees levied on British citizens for wills, inventories and other documents related to property transfers.

The colonies hated the stamp acts of the British. But the Congress of the fledgling United States of America copied the British and came out with their own version of the hated law with the Stamp Act of 1797. It was a desperate measure to raise money to pay for an undeclared war with France.

From the perspective of many business owners, stamp acts boiled down to government extortion. If you want to legalize this or that document, or sell this or that product, you must pay the tax imposed. Don't pay the tax, and your paperwork will not be stamped as valid by the government, and your transaction, or your business, will be null and void. The Stamp Act of 1797 had several vocal opponents and was repealed in 1802.

It came back under another name as the Revenue Act of 1862, a measure passed to tax estates left to heirs. The purpose of that legislation was to help pay for the Civil War. This legislation was also vehemently opposed and was abolished in 1870.

Estates of the deceased were again taxed under the War Revenue Act of 1898. It was abolished in 1902 after the debt incurred for the Spanish-American War had been paid off.

Up until the time of World War I, it seems that a "death tax" would be levied to pay for a war and then lifted when the war debt had been repaid. Then along came the Revenue Act of 1916 to pay the **anticipated** cost of World War I. This one did not go away. America's current estate tax is based on this law, which, in some fashion, is still in force. At the time of this writing, estates of under $5.12 million are exempt. But the exemption is a year-by-year thing and leaves planners scratching their heads as to what the future holds. It is like the blade of an axe, suspended for now, but capable of a vicious downswing at any time.

Some politicians say they want to keep the estate tax under control with legislative provisions intended to create more fairness in the exist-

ing law. Those who oppose the estate tax say "don't mend it, end it."
Why would anyone favor the tax, you ask? Proponents say it won't hurt
the economy because it only affects a small fraction of the population.
They say that the heirs won't miss the money — they're wealthy anyway.
They maintain the estate tax is a way to break up unfair concentrations
of wealth and redistribute it.

I think you know by now where I stand on this issue. True, the estate
tax may break up unfair concentrations of wealth, but it does it rather
poorly since it does so at the expense of capital growth. What's more, as
taxes go, the death tax produces little revenue — I don't think it's nearly
the amount that would be generated if the same amount were pumped
into private enterprise. People tend to respond to incentives. Where's
the incentive here? The incentive is to avoid accumulation, eschew saving and stop investing.

I can't help it if, from time to time, you read of some rich heiress
spending her way across three continents with money she didn't earn
and still could never fritter away her billions if she had eight lifetimes.
That just goes with the territory of being rich. She is helping the economy by her shopping sprees. Look how many merchants she keeps in
business.

Come to think about it, even that problem would be solved if taxation were to be based on spending, instead of working and saving.

Alas, just wishing away the estate tax won't eliminate it, I'm afraid. It
seems to have staying power. But as a financial advisor, my job is to help
clients who do not wish to participate in such a tax find legal and ethical
ways of "disinheriting" the government. There are laws on the books if
you know where to find them, and strategies in place, if you know how
they work, that will accomplish that purpose in most instances. I enjoy
working with my clients' estate planning attorneys to help them use
their trusts, helping them place their funds in a "multi-generational status" that bypasses the death tax altogether. The goal is to use all the provisions made available by the federal government to keep Uncle Sam's
fingers out of places where they don't belong. Strategies are available
that will allow people with IRAs to stretch their inheritance to their

grandchildren and, in many cases, great-grandchildren, thereby keeping their money, like any other valuable possession, inside the family and away from the clutches of the "estate tax monster."

The "Senior Only" Tax

You will hear different versions of this — and no one who was actually there that day is talking — but it is claimed that in 1935, when FDR signed Social Security into law, a crowd of reporters asked him if he would ever tax Social Security benefits. The story goes that he pounded his fist on the table and proclaimed, "I will never tax Social Security!"

The Social Security Administration says he never uttered those words. Even if he didn't, the promise was kept. As long as President Roosevelt was alive, there was no tax imposed on Social Security benefits. That dubious honor would ultimately belong to two other chief executives, William Jefferson Clinton and Ronald Reagan.

It would be the Social Security Amendments of 1983, when Ronald Reagan was president, that would, for the first time since the days of FDR, require a tax on Social Security benefits. The law was enacted in 1983 and it took effect in 1984, meaning if your base annual income was $25,000 as a single taxpayer or $32,000 as a married couple filing jointly, then up to 50 percent of your Social Security income would be treated as taxable income.

The 1993 budget deal under President Clinton raised taxation to up to 85 percent of benefits for single beneficiaries with incomes over $34,000, and couples earning more than $44,000. So how do you get around that? It's the law, right?

Keep in mind the taxes on Social Security benefits hinge on how much you earn in the way of *reportable* income each year. Reportable income includes:

- Income from pensions
- Income from investments, such as stocks and mutual funds
- Income from bank CDs
- Income from tax-free municipal bonds (yes, it's true)

If your modified adjusted gross income, plus one-half of your combined Social Security benefits, plus any tax-exempt interest you receive (your combined income) is above the limit, then sorry, Charlie. You will be taxed accordingly.

Will the thresholds be moved again? Could even more of your Social Security be taxed in the future? Well, incomes have risen since 1993. Social Security benefits have risen since 1993. I think it is unlikely that the tax will ever be reduced or eliminated; it is more likely it will be raised.

Oh yes. How to avoid paying these taxes. First, I must tell you a little joke I like to throw into my remarks about this when I speak at income planning seminars. It goes like this: "Does anyone know what the difference is between *tax evasion* and *tax avoidance?* About 10 to 20 years."

There are perfectly legitimate and perfectly legal ways to avoid paying more than your fair share of income taxes. One way is to simply place assets in tax-deferred accounts; the IRS doesn't consider interest you receive from those kind of accounts as current taxable income, and is therefore not reportable. Interest you earn on annuity balances, for example, are tax-deferred and are not reported as income on 1040 forms. This is not the case with interest earned by CDs and gains from mutual funds. They are fully reportable and taxable each year.

Make no mistake… you will *eventually* pay taxes on annuity interest. Tax-deferred means taxes are postponed. But the more income you can move to the *unreportable* side of the tax return form, the further away you stand from Social Security taxation.

I advise anyone considering making such changes to first consult with a tax professional. This is because every case is different, and the tax professional can inform you accurately as to whether such a move is in your best interest.

The Phantom Income Menace

What is phantom income? Sounds scary, doesn't it? It can be if it prompts unnecessary taxes. Phantom income is defined as income that has been reported to the IRS *as if* you received it, but you never saw it and didn't spend it. If you own equities and you sell off shares of those holdings at a profit without actually pulling those profits from the account, do you owe taxes on those gains? Yes.

"But hold on a minute," you protest. "I just left the money in the account!" Sorry, Uncle Sam doesn't care. You owe him taxes on those gains.

Some people don't take this very well. One man attending a financial seminar I conducted said he needed an appointment right away, so I obliged him. It turns out he was an engineer. He told me in quite colorful language that he would like to wring his accountant's neck.

Most engineers with whom I am acquainted are detail-oriented. They like to know where their money goes and strive to understand the nuts and bolts of financial products and strategies. I could tell this man was frustrated. Something just didn't add up to him.

The man, who had brought his checkbook and his tax returns with him, proceeded to show me how that he had been paid the same salary every two weeks for all of the previous year.

"This tax guy doesn't know what he is doing," he said, pointing to the documents. "Here, let me show you exactly what I made last year."

He had recorded every salary deposit in his checkbook and had balanced it down to the penny. He had made exactly $100,000 the year before. On his tax return, however, it showed him making $110,000!

"See… my tax guy doesn't know what he's doing," he said, handing me the return.

After perusing the document for a minute or two, I said, "Unfortunately, he does know what he's doing. You have some phantom income here."

With mutual funds, you have a manager whose job it is to keep your fund properly allocated. This means that he may make several stock trades a year, trying to buy what he considers good stocks, or stocks that will make the portfolio grow, and sell off the ones that he considers losers. If the fund manager sells any of those stocks within the portfolio at a profit, it is credited to you as income. But it is **phantom** income. You never saw the money. It never entered your checking account. You did not withdraw the profit. You left it in the mutual fund. But the IRS rule is that you pay taxes on it anyway. I explained this to the engineer.

"That's why it shows up on your tax return that you made $110,000 in income instead of $100,000," I told him.

There was a pause.

"That's still the craziest thing I've ever heard of," he said.

We set a second appointment, at which time we reviewed his entire financial situation and found ways — perfectly legal, ethical and legitimate — to eliminate this tax. In fact, we were able to use provisions the IRS has placed there for us all to use. It's right there in the Internal Revenue Code. It's in perfectly readable type and is clearly written. But it's not advertised, and, unfortunately, there is no chapter entitled *Tax Breaks* in the IRS code book.

You may call them tax "loopholes" if you want to, but they aren't. They are "IRS provisions," a more accurate and less reprehensible term. And you have to look for them. They won't jump off the page, curtsy and introduce themselves.

Double Taxation in IRA Distributions

This one may not affect you while you are living, but if you die and pass the value of an IRA on to your heirs as part of your estate, not only will your estate be hit with taxes, but your heirs will be taxed again when they take their required minimum distributions, or RMDs, from the account. They will, in fact, have to pay ordinary income tax on the amounts that are distributed.

Failure to track the "basis" in an IRA can also cause you tax problems. Ask your financial advisor about this one.

Municipal Bond Interest

Cautious, tax-averse investors love municipal bonds, because "they're tax-free!"

Well, yes and no. There are all kinds of taxes. There is state tax, federal tax, income tax, sales tax, property tax, gasoline tax, corporate tax, estate tax, etc. It is true that U.S. government bonds are free from state and local taxes. Municipal bonds are free from federal taxes, but you may owe state taxes on them if the bonds were not issued by the state in which you live.

With traditional bonds, it's pretty straightforward. They pay annual interest, which is usually taxed. But what of zero-coupon bonds where no interest is paid? The bond holder will still be presented with a statement of *imputed* interest. This is sometimes called "phantom interest." The amount of imputed interest you are credited with is based on the eventual realized gain, broken down over the life of the bond. Yes, this imputed interest is then taxed each year, just like interest from a traditional bond. The drawback of a zero-coupon bond is you have to pay taxes on "phantom" income (price appreciation) while you are holding it.

IRC Thicker than "War and Peace"

You will probably never understand all the provisions made by the Internal Revenue Code. When people want to name a book that is notoriously long and difficult to read, they will inevitably mention Leo Tolstoy's "War and Peace," which contains 1,440 pages in its paperback edition. Marcell Proust's "In Search of Lost Time" holds the record for thick novels, weighing in at a whopping 4,211 pages.

The IRC book, however, beats that all to pieces! It took government compilers 7,500 pages and 3.4 million words to explain the Internal Revenue Code! Not to worry, however, because there are paid professionals at your disposal who have made it their job to understand it. There are entire computer programs and complicated search engines dedicated to ferreting out any of its provisions that may work to your advantage.

CHAPTER 4

S-t-r-e-t-c-h Your IRA
Before It's Too Late

When I am scheduled to conduct a financial seminar on retirement, I like to poll the audience and ask, "How many here have an IRA?" Most of the time, about half of the people raise their hand. Nationally, 33 percent of all Americans own an IRA.[3]

There are several kinds of IRAs. The most common is the **traditional IRA.** A traditional IRA is usually held at a custodian institution, such as a bank or a brokerage house. They are often invested in certificates of deposit, stocks or mutual funds. Traditional IRAs are pretty straightforward when it comes to taxes. Earnings are not subject to taxation while they remain in the account, but they are taxed upon withdrawal.

The other type of IRA, the Roth IRA, is named for Sen. William Roth of Delaware, who pioneered the creation of an IRA that would allow taxes to be paid upfront, investments to grow tax-free and to be withdrawn tax-free at retirement. Roth accounts are about taxing the seed instead of the harvest, so to speak. Put another way, your contributions to a Roth account are made with after-tax dollars; so, since you have already paid taxes, your investments will grow sans taxes, and your

---

[3] TIAA. June 29, 2016. "Most Americans Don't See a Difference Among IRAs." https://www.tiaa.org/public/about-tiaa/news-press/press-releases/pressrelease647.html.

qualified withdrawals/any withdrawals you make after age 59 ½ will also be tax-free. Of course, if this is a strategy you are considering for retirement, you may want to be aware that Roth accounts also have a provision that says you have to have owned the account for at least five years to be able to make your tax-free withdrawals.

The Birth of IRAs

The Peabody Award-winning 1972 NBC News documentary entitled "Pensions: The Broken Promise" woke up the nation. It focused national attention on some pension plans that were poorly funded, poorly managed or outright fraudulent. Narrator Edwin Newman interviewed several people who had worked for decades and were expecting to receive a lifetime payout when they retired, only to find out they had been lied to. Financial professionals, historians and policy wonks cite this documentary more than any other single thing as being the mobilizing force that led to the development of IRAs in 1974 when President Gerald Ford signed the Employee Retirement Income Security Act (ERISA) into law.

The primary function of ERISA was to regulate pension plans, how they were operated, and how they paid out their benefits. A side benefit, however, was the creation of the IRA. IRAs allow you to contribute a certain amount every pay period to a special account and let the money grow tax-deferred. It didn't take Americans long to spot this as a good deal. Not only did what you saved in this account grow, but the cash you would have paid in taxes grew, too.

The government got a good deal as well. They figured that this would encourage people to save for retirement, which it did. What did the government care if taxes were not paid right away? They were content to wait until the IRA accounts grew nice and fat, and collect their taxes then. Look at how much more they would collect in taxes in 20 or 30 years. It was a win-win situation.

Inherited IRAs

Where it gets complicated is when the IRA owner dies and passes the value of the account on to heirs, who then face a potential double tax hit. First, if the deceased owner's estate is large enough to meet the federal estate tax threshold, the IRA will be subject to federal estate tax. Second, payments from the IRA to other beneficiaries are subject to income taxes.

If you inherit an IRA from a spouse, you have special privileges that you wouldn't have if you were to inherit it from someone else, like an uncle, aunt or parent. A spousal beneficiary has several options. You may:

- **Roll it over.** If you have an IRA of your own, you can roll the inherited IRA proceeds into your existing IRA. You may even create a new IRA with the proceeds and continue contributing to it. Non-spousal beneficiaries aren't allowed to roll over inherited IRA funds, and they cannot add contributions to an inherited IRA.

- **Remain a beneficiary.** If you do this, then the IRA becomes what is called a "beneficiary distribution account." Both your name and the name of your deceased spouse remain on the account. If you, as the surviving spouse, are younger than 59 ½, you can tap funds from the IRA without paying a 10 percent penalty.

- **Cash out the account.** You can do this, but I don't usually recommend it because it will trigger a taxable event. Talk to a tax professional before you do this, please.

- **Give it away.** If you are financially well-off and don't need the money, you may choose to give the inherited IRA to a child, for example. The account can continue growing tax-deferred. I suggest that you seek the advice of an attorney before you do this one.

Non-spousal inheritances

First, only a spouse can commingle funds with other IRAs. If you inherit an IRA from one of your parents, for example, you have to keep it separate. Also, you aren't allowed to make new contributions to it. Do you think you might inherit an IRA from someone other than your spouse? Then it may be advantageous to do some planning. The rules regarding designating beneficiaries are a little tricky. It would be wise to get with a financial advisor who specializes in retirement income planning and who knows the ins and outs of IRAs.

When it comes to IRA beneficiaries, you want to list a living, breathing, named person. While you can just put down "my estate," I can almost guarantee that you don't want to. Why? Well, IRAs and their required distributions and policies are all based on the policy owner's life expectancy. If the policy owner is your estate or your trust, tell me, when will your estate reach maturity? How old will your trust live to be? Remember that IRA stands for *individual* retirement account. Naming a non-individual as the owner or beneficiary of your policy means that, as soon as the ownership transfers to that non-individual, it is no longer an *individual* retirement account. Essentially, transferring it this way takes all of the funds out of their tax-protected IRA wrapper, meaning your estate will have to pay the 10 percent early withdrawal tax penalty (after all, your estate hasn't turned 59 ½), as well as income taxes and any other fees. Instead, most people prefer to name a person as a designated beneficiary.

If you directly inherit an IRA as a designated beneficiary, you have choices on how to handle the withdrawals. This is a good thing. This is where the term "stretch" comes in. You can stretch out the distributions over your own life expectancy, as measured by the government's life expectancy table.

Explaining the S-t-r-e-t-c-h

To most people, stretching is something they usually do while yawning or before running. Few people associate it with tax rules that allow you to position an IRA so you can create a legacy for future generations while protecting them from burdensome and unfair taxes. At the seminars where I explain this area of financial planning, the conversation may go something like this:

"How many here own an IRA? Can see a show of hands?"

Half the hands go up.

"Would you like to know how you can greatly reduce a huge tax that will be imposed on your IRA when you die?"

Several affirmative nods. A few verbal yeses.

"First of all, women typically outlive men by a few years, so let's illustrate it this way. Let's say a husband leaves an IRA to his wife. She rolls it over into her own IRA. Then a few years later she dies. By now it is worth $250,000. She leaves it to her son, Junior, who makes $50,000 per year. Junior is notified by the custodians of the IRA that was owned by his parents. They tell him that they are sending him a check for a quarter of a million dollars. To this point has any of this money ever been taxed?"

Someone in the crowd: "No."

"That's right. This money has never seen the light of day as far as taxes are concerned. So when Junior inherits $250,000, it is added to his income as if he earned it on the job that year."

Someone in the crowd: "Uh-oh."

"Uh-oh is right. That means he pays the maximum tax possible, right? Now, mom and dad were both savers. Junior is not inclined that way. He's a spender. How long do you think it will take Junior to run through his inheritance?

Someone in the crowd: "About two weeks." (Laughter)

"In any case, let's say Junior puts the money in a CD at the bank. Then, when it comes tax time, he goes to see the accountant. The accountant looks at his documents and explains to him that he owes taxes on his $50,000 salary at work, and also on the $250,000 he inherited. And Junior says, 'Wait a minute...what do you mean?'

"The accountant goes on to explain to him that because of the inheritance, he is in the highest tax bracket for both federal and state income taxes and will have to pay 40 percent of the money to the government. That's around $100,000.

"Now you are the ones who scraped and saved all your lives to build that IRA. How many of you are in a happy place right now?"

No hands go up.

"Now let's talk about Publication 590 in the IRS Codebook. This came out in April of 2002 and if you haven't heard of it, then you need to. Pub 590 allows us to take your ordinary IRA and make it a *multigenerational IRA*."

A hand goes up. "What is a multigenerational IRA?"

Another hand goes up. "What's a 'Pub 590?"

"Those are excellent questions. When it comes to retirement accounts, Publication 590 is the rule book. It tells you everything from contribution limits to taxes. It's over 100 pages long. A **multigenerational IRA** is the same thing as a 'stretch IRA.' Some call it a 'legacy IRA.'

"If you set up your beneficiaries properly, you can stretch the tax-deferred status of the IRA out for decades to come. But in order to get the maximum benefits with the least possible tax consequences, what I'm about to say is important. *You have to fill out the form just so.* Please don't guess at this, folks. The language on the beneficiary page has to agree word for word with IRS rules for it to work. Don't worry. If this is something that would work well for your situation, I can help you with this. But, yes, you will probably want to leave it to the kids and grandkids, and maybe even great-grandchildren if they are around. Does anybody here have children or grandchildren?"

Heads nod. A few hands go up.

"Anybody have great-grandchildren?"

Heads nod again.

"Great! If you name them specifically as your beneficiaries, you enable them to stretch out the annual distributions from that IRA over the course of their lifetimes. Remember Junior? How much did he have to pay in taxes without the stretch?

Someone says, "$100,000."

"But with a little planning, his parents could have structured the IRA so that he would only withdraw the required minimum distribution based on his age. Let's say that RMD was around $6,000. That's all he would have to pay taxes on. He gets to invest the rest and let it continue to grow, tax-deferred."

The Golden Rule

You have probably heard the adage about following the "golden rule." Growing up, it was, "Do unto others as you would have them do unto you." Well, in this modern day world of taxes and IRS rules and regulations, at least when it comes to getting the most out of an IRA, the golden rule goes like this: "Whoever has the gold makes the rules!"

The IRS has the gold, and they make the rules. They are playing the fiddle, and we have to dance to their tune. This is especially true when it comes to filing the proper forms to meet our objective, which is to allow our children and grandchildren to be able to take advantage of our hard work, diligent saving and investing strategies, not fill Uncle Sam's coffers with it.

I have seen hundreds of cases where people inherited IRAs from parents and had no idea about stretch provisions. They often discover that stretching the IRA after it is inherited is complicated and sometimes impossible, whereas, had a little planning been done while the parents were still living, much confusion and unnecessary taxation could have been eliminated.

Some Things to Remember

Here are some things to remember about inherited IRAs:
- If you inherit an IRA, the money must be moved from one IRA custodian to another. If you are dealing with your own IRA, you can take the money out and redeposit it into another IRA, let it

sit in your checking account for a few days (no more than 60 days) and then redeposit it into another IRA without causing a taxable event. Not with an inherited IRA. You need to make sure that it is a "trustee-to-trustee" transfer.

- Unless you are a spouse inheriting an IRA from your deceased spouse, you have to rename the IRA, including the original owner's name and indicating that it is inherited. For example, "Daisy Duck, deceased, inherited IRA for the benefit of Louie Duck, beneficiary." Like I said. It's tricky. Don't guess at this. See a professional.

- If more than one person is named as a beneficiary, ask the custodian to separate the funds. One beneficiary may wish to handle his affairs in a different manner than another. This avoids disputes later on.

- It is the "designated beneficiary form" on file with the custodian of an IRA that determines who inherits an IRA, not a will. This form, and how it is filled out, also determines whether the IRA can be stretched.

- If someone other than a spouse is named beneficiary, they have to begin taking required minimum distributions from the account by Dec. 31 of the year after they inherit the account.

- If you want your heirs to have flexibility, it is a good idea to name both primary and alternate beneficiaries. Let's say that your spouse is primary beneficiary and the children are alternates. Your spouse can, if he or she wishes, "disclaim" the account and pass it along to one or more of the children.

- If you pass on a Roth IRA, all funds have to be taken out within five years.

As you would expect from anything designed, produced and directed by the government, there are complexities to the rules that require a magnifying glass and a steady hand to read, and an insightful mind to understand and apply. We have made a dent in it here and covered some basics, but please remember that every case is different and requires individual scrutiny before a decision can or should be made. There are a lot of what-ifs you will want to review with your financial advisor and tax professional before doing anything.

CHAPTER 5

Understanding Bubbles and Market Crashes

I believe human emotion causes all movements in the stock market —
mainly fear and greed. Investors begin pumping buy orders into
stocks, causing prices to escalate higher and higher. Some worry
they will be left behind, so they rush the market with even more buy
orders. Greed can drive up the price beyond any true reflection of its
actual value. If it weren't for the emotions involved, the value of a company's stock would be determined by the company's performance and
profits. But then again, that's why it called a market, isn't it? Something
is worth whatever someone else is willing to pay for it.

Like soap bubbles, the kind we blew when we were children, market
bubbles often soar upward as if they would rise forever. But inevitably,
they pop. Fear sets in. Those who were afraid they were going to be too
late to the party often scramble for the exits. They withdraw their money from investments. Stock values might drop as these investors rush to
sell in an attempt to avoid being a victim of the landslide. In the worst-
case scenarios (ever heard of the Great Depression?), panic selling en-
sues. Investors hope to unload their declining stocks onto other investors, but there are few takers. While the market is seldom this unsteady,
I think it's fair to say market bubbles end in market drops, with recessions following on the heels of those large market crashes.

It is similar to the way clouds and rain are related. You can have
clouds without rain, but you can't have rain without clouds. Bubbles are

like clouds and stock market crashes are like the rain. The thicker the clouds (or, the bigger the bubble), the harder it rains.

Sometimes the optimists and market cheerleaders want to put bright, sunny labels on bad news. They would prefer to say that the market is "correcting." But there is a significant difference between a market "crash" and a market "correction." A correction is a naturally occurring phenomenon whereby overly aggressive investors who lack caution have their wrists slapped by a downturn. Most experts view a market dip of less than 20 percent as a "correction." Media characterization of such a downward movement of the market may be influenced by how rapidly the market recovers. News writers turn up the rhetoric considerably when the losses cross the 20 percent line and stay there for an extended period. The talking heads on television begin to toss out such terms as "tailspin" and "spiraling." Headlines will include words like "stock market tumble" and "freefall." The word "crash" seems to be reserved for more catastrophic reversals when losses are sudden, sustained and well past the 20 percent mark. The general mood of the public is also a factor. A quick bounce back will brighten a bleak mood and tone down the rhetoric.

The 1987 Crash

For some reason, members of the media have tended to label the crash of Oct. 19, 1987, as a correction. But it was a crash. Oct. 19, 1987, saw the largest single-day drop in the history of the market up to that point — 508 points. The market rallied quickly, but did not regain the perch from which it fell until two years later.

Several factors converged to cause the 1987 crash. For one thing, the 1980s marked the emergence of the computer. Trading programs began to surface that allowed savvy investors to manipulate the market. Also, insider trading was investigated by the Securities and Exchange Commission, and a five-year bull market was at the end of its run. Whatever the cause, 500 billion dollars vaporized in one fell swoop. No matter how you shake it, it was a whopper.

The Dot-Com Bubble

Decades before we ever uttered the words "dot-com," a computer network was developed by the U.S. military. They had no idea what would eventually happen once the technology went public. The Internet became commercially available in the late 1980s and soared to popularity. By 1995, this strange and exciting technological wonder had captured almost 20 million users in its "web" (pun intended) and had begun to create a new economy. Investors saw this rise in popularity as a new business opportunity with untapped potential. Computer manufacturers couldn't make enough of the machines, and any business connected with this new wave was thought to be a sure success. Initial public offerings, or IPOs, of new Internet companies popped up like dandelions after a rain. Investors were in a feeding frenzy, grabbing at every new issue without even checking the business plan to see how long it would take for the company to become profitable. As the Commander Jim Lovell said after an explosion crippled the Apollo 13 spacecraft in deep space, "Uh... Houston, we have a problem."

While owners of these fledgling Internet companies were becoming gazillionaires overnight, many of the companies themselves reported huge losses, floundered and then sank within months of going public. In 1999, 457 IPOs hit the streets. Nearly all of them were Internet-related. By 2001, there were only 76 IPOs offering stock, and they were fast losing appeal. The chickens were in a landing pattern, coming home to roost.

From March 11, 2000, to Oct. 9, 2002, the Nasdaq Composite, an exchange comprised primarily of technology stocks, lost 78 percent of its value, falling from 5046.86 to 1114.11. The human emotions of greed and fear were again major causes of the dot-com bust. Each new Internet business wanted to monopolize its sector, and competition was so fierce that many of the companies couldn't make it. Investors who once couldn't wait to get in the tech market now couldn't wait to get out.

The Nasdaq, which began trading on Feb. 8, 1971, was the world's first electronic stock market. Like the mythical Icarus, who dared to fly too close to the sun on wings of feathers and wax, the Nasdaq soared too high too quickly, and so came crashing down. On March 2, 2015, the Nasdaq Composite Index again closed at over 5,000. Back to square one after 15 years? Yes, but it wasn't the same Nasdaq. In an article that appeared in *The New York Times* three days later, market analyst James B. Stewart pointed out that only three companies that were among the top 10 in 2000 were there for its hallmark recovery — Microsoft, Cisco and Intel. About the others, Stewart writes: "Eight no longer exist as independent companies, most as a result of bankruptcy or acquisition, and several are shadows of their former selves. The current Nasdaq composite index has only about half as many companies as it did in 2000."

The Market Crash of 2008

I sometimes wish we treated stock market catastrophes the way we do hurricanes, earthquakes and tornados. We assign a category number to natural disasters. You may stay home for a category two hurricane, for example, but you will evacuate for a category five. With hurricanes, we even give them names, alternating through the alphabet, male and female — Alice, Bob, Christine, Danny, etc.

As economic catastrophes go, the market crash of 2008 was an earthquake measuring 8.5 on the Richter scale, a category five hurricane and a tsunami all rolled into one. The record 508-point drop that occurred on "Black Monday" in 1987 was easily shattered almost 21 years later on Sept. 29, 2008, by the largest point drop ever recorded. The Dow Jones Industrial Average closed down 777.68 points, losing 6.98 percent in one day. There would be no quick bounce back this time. The Dow fell again on Oct. 15, losing 733.08 points, a 7.87 percent loss, according to the Wall Street Journal Historical Index.

Things began to fall apart when Lehman Brothers Investment Bank issued the largest bankruptcy protection filing in history. In hindsight, however, economists say the credit crisis that put Wall Street on its derriere was the culmination of 10 years of poor banking policies. Things actually began coming to a head a year before the Lehman Brothers collapse. The entire banking system had been infected with easy home loans obtained by unqualified buyers, issued by banks that were willing to believe home values would continue climbing into infinity. Water began seeping through the cracks in the dam when property values started to slide in 2007. Millions of homeowners were soon in over their heads, with loans that exceeded what their homes were worth. It turned out to be the largest housing bubble in history with the loudest pop ever recorded when it burst.

The casualty list of the 2008 market disaster would soon grow to include such giants as Bear Stearns, Fannie Mae (the Federal National Mortgage Association) and Freddy Mac (the Federal Home Loan Mortgage Corporation). Even the international banking giant, American International Group (AIG) would join the list, having reported a $13.2 billion loss. Merrill Lynch, another pillar of the banking community, would be bought by Bank of America at a discount, permanently losing its Wall Street identity.

The severity of the 2008 crash would be defined by eight consecutive trading days in October that would see the Dow fall 2,399.47 points, or 22.11 percent. Some investors saw as much as half their life savings go "poof," like dandelion dust in the wind. The recession that followed would be the longest and deepest in history and would drive the unemployment rate up to 10 percent by October 2009.

The Human Cost

As a financial advisor, I was privy to a front row seat for the Great Recession of 2008. I work mainly with seniors who are approaching retirement, and with a few who have already retired. I am a proponent of conservative investing, and while my clients were fairly insulated from the 2008 bloodletting, I spoke to many prospective clients who didn't fare so well. They told me how it affected them personally.

"We had one more year to go before retirement," one couple told me. "We lost around nearly half of our retirement savings."

The couple had planned to sell their home and move to a cottage near the beach. Those plans had to be put on indefinite hold. They said they were forced to rethink their retirement strategy completely. When the housing bubble burst, they lost more than $80,000 equity in their paid-for home, making relocating impossible.

Statistically, in 2008 and 2009, the American public lost a whopping 53 percent of its wealth. According to CNNMoney, the Great Recession cost Americans $16.4 trillion. Markets may rebound — the wealth lost in the last market dive has been regained, plus more — yet, it's not always about a straight dollar-for-dollar calculation. In human terms, the losses are difficult to measure. A nest egg can be rebuilt, but time cannot be regained. Like those who survive a natural disaster and have to pick up the pieces of their lives, many of those whose dreams were shattered by the crash of 2008 and the ensuing recession are still reeling from the psychological fallout.

"What do we do now?" asked one man who saw most of his savings washed away.

It was a rhetorical question. He didn't really expect an answer. But I thought about the question long after our interview had concluded.

"We do what we have always done," I should have told him. "We pick up the pieces. We learn from our mistakes and try not to repeat them. We carry on."

CHAPTER 6

Safe is the New Sexy for Seniors

More and more Americans who are approaching retirement are less and less willing to gamble with their life savings in a volatile stock market. They no longer trust the spiels of brokers whose hollow mantras of, "just hang in there; it will come back" simply do not ring true anymore. The events after 2008 have taught these older Americans a valuable lesson in economics — two steps forward and three steps back is still going backward. Many have gotten off the roller coaster and do not want any more wild rides. Their investing goals are different now. Their aim is to realize reasonable, consistent gains while preserving the assets they already have. If 60 is the new 40, then *safe* seems to be the new *sexy* for seniors.

Risk Tolerance

I grew up in DeKalb, Illinois, where the freight trains of the Union Pacific Railroad rumbled through the flat town at speeds in excess of 60 miles per hour. I remember seeing young boys play a game of "chicken" with the locomotive, standing on the tracks with the train approaching and jumping off just in the nick of time. I never joined them. The idea still makes me shudder. Such behavior was way too risky for conservative me.

Whenever I hear the term, "risk tolerance," I think of those stupid kids on that railroad track taunting the train. What if their reflexes had been slow? What if they had misjudged the speed of the train? What if they tripped when stepping out of the way? It still gives me the shivers.

When it comes to investing, everyone has a particular risk tolerance, and it is the job of every competent financial advisor to determine what that tolerance level is for every new client. This is one reason I make it a practice to listen far more than I talk on the first interview with any prospective client. After all, it's their money. Only they know what they want it to do for them. My job is to help them accomplish their goals.

Educators who study investing risk tolerance develop surveys for the purpose of pegging it on a scale. Two university personal finance professors, Ruth Lytton, Ph.D., at Virginia Tech and John Grable, Ph.D., at Kansas State University, came up with some interesting questions to help gauge risk tolerance levels. I've included a sample of them.

Age is Critical Factor

Again, this is just a sampling. The complete survey developed by Grable and Lytton contains 20 questions and, toward the end, poses what I think are the most pertinent questions: How old are you? When do you plan to retire?

One of the questions on the Grable-Lytton survey could be answered quite differently by a young, adventurous person versus someone approaching or in retirement. The question asks, *"Your trusted friend and neighbor, an experienced geologist, is putting together a group of investors to fund an exploratory gold mining venture. The venture could pay back 50 to 100 times the investment if successful. If the mine is a bust, the entire investment is worthless. Your friend estimates the chance of success is only 20 percent. If you had the money, how much would you invest?"*

- Nothing
- One month's salary
- Three month's salary
- Six month's salary

1. **In general, how would your best friend describe you as a risk-taker?**

   ❏ A real gambler   ❏ Willing to take risks after completing adequate research
   ❏ Cautious   ❏ A real risk avoider

2. **You are on a TV game show and can choose one of the following. Which would you take?**

   ❏ $1,000 in cash
   ❏ A 50 percent chance at winning $5,000
   ❏ A 25 percent chance at winning $10,000
   ❏ A 5 percent chance at winning $100,000

3. **You have just finished saving for a "once-in-a-lifetime" vacation. Three weeks before you plan to leave, you lose your job. You would:**

   ❏ Cancel the vacation.
   ❏ Take a much more modest vacation.
   ❏ Go as scheduled, reasoning that you need the time to prepare for a job search.
   ❏ Extend your vacation, because this might be your last chance to go first-class.

4. **If you unexpectedly received $20,000 to invest, what would you do?**

   ❏ Deposit it in a bank account, money market account or an insured CD.
   ❏ Invest it in safe, high-quality bonds or bond mutual funds.
   ❏ Invest it in stocks or stock mutual funds.

5. **In terms of experience, how comfortable are you investing in stocks or stock mutual funds?**

   ❏ Not at all comfortable   ❏ Somewhat comfortable
   ❏ Very comfortable

6. **When you think of the word "risk" which of the following words comes to mind first?**

   ❏ Loss   ❏ Uncertainty
   ❏ Opportunity   ❏ Thrill

Hey, If I'm 25 years old and earning $3,000 a month, I might throw a few dollars on that deal. After all, he is my trusted friend, and he lives next door. And he is a geologist, for crying out loud. If I'm lucky, I could get back, what? $150,000? $300,000? My pal next door is just being conservative when he says there is only a 20 percent chance of success. Why would he be risking his relationship with me and all his other friends if it weren't a pretty good deal? Right?

But if I am approaching retirement and I am earning $7,000 per month, I would probably invest nothing. Values change as we grow older. We are less likely to take chances by nature, not only with our money, but with our health and our physical activity.

I am not picking on any financial advisor group when I say this, but brokers should ask the following question of their clients who are nearing retirement, "The money that you have, how much of it do you want to lose?" And they should ask it just that way, too. It puts things in perspective. Don't sugarcoat it with possible rewards. After all, those rewards are only *possible* rewards. After the events of 2008, it should be evident that no one who advocates that retirees invest large portions of their life savings in the stock market has a crystal ball. If they did, when they saw a crash coming they would surely have the professional courtesy to call their clients who are nearing retirement to tell them that are on the railroad tracks, and the train is coming.

The point is, no one knows. So the question once again is, "How much of your money do you want to lose?"

If the answer they receive is "None!" then that financial advisor has an obligation to assess that individual's risk tolerance as zero and advise them accordingly.

Brokers live and work in a world of risk and reward. Their pitch is, "no risk, no reward. No pain, no gain." If you are a conservative investor who doesn't want to lose any your money, then your first question should be, "If you put this much of my money in this or that position in the market, how much of it could I possibly lose?"

Your second question should be, "What are the tax implications?"

In earlier chapters, we discussed "phantom income" and the "phantom taxes" that result from it. This is an important piece of information to know. When it comes to retirement income planning, the difference between tax-favored money and non-tax-favored money is huge.

Your third question should be, "If I draw an income, will I experience the effect known as 'reverse dollar cost averaging'?"

Reverse Dollar Cost Averaging

What is "reverse dollar cost averaging"? Say when you were younger and still in the accumulation stage of life, you were making regular, systematic contributions into an investment portfolio. You benefited from "dollar cost averaging."

If the stock market was up, then wonderful! The balance in your retirement savings account was up, too. If the market was down, wonderful! Share prices were lower. Your regular contributions bought more shares at bargain prices. Time was on your side.

Things change when you retire. In fact, it's the reverse side of the coin. Let's say now you are making withdrawals from the same retirement portfolio. Those periodic declines in the price of shares no longer work in your favor because you are selling off shares to provide income, in fact, it is now detrimental to you. When the share price goes down, you have to sell more shares to obtain the amount of money you need just to pay bills and stay alive.

Let's say that you have a portfolio worth $1 million, and in that portfolio you have 100,000 shares valued at $10 per share. Let's also assume that you need $50,000 per year in income. If the stock is worth $10 per share, then you need to sell 5,000 shares to produce the income needed. What if the share prices drop to $6? Now you need to sell 8,333 shares to raise the same amount.

You have just been the victim of "reverse dollar cost averaging."

The Sequence of Returns Trap

"Don't worry about all that," your broker-dealer may say. "Long term, the market always produces a 10 percent return."

While historically that may be accurate, we can't know the future. And, in your case, as a retiree, depending on this account for your income, it is a non sequitur. It might be okay if you were a buy-and-hold investor, but you aren't. Your portfolio is a retirement portfolio, under the constant stress of systematic withdrawals. There is something called "sequence of returns" to be considered.

Sequence of returns is the **order** in which returns are realized. You can have an unfavorable sequence of returns early in retirement, and it can throw you into serious jeopardy down the road. As we established earlier, selling off shares when prices are low leads to a premature depletion of the account. So if timing is that important, don't talk to me about long-term if I am in a position of having to sell shares on a regular basis to produce an income. Sure, there may be an average of 10 percent return in a 20-year period, but those years when stock prices are down by 30 percent are a killer. I would have to sell off so much just to make ends meet that I would be unable to take advantage of the years when share prices recovered. Timing is everything, sometimes, and if you are dealing with a retirement portfolio, time just isn't always on your side.

Use the Rule of 100

Wouldn't it be great if there was some kind of formula that would tell me how much of my money should be at risk in the market and how much should be entirely safe?

Well, there is. It's called the "Rule of 100." Take your age and subtract it from 100. That's the percentage of your assets you may have at risk.

Another way to figure it is by putting a percent sign after your age. That is the percentage of your money that you may have, and often should have, completely safe, altogether free from market risk.

Now, the Rule of 100 is not actually a hardline rule; think of it more as a ballpark figure, a starting point. There are a lot of different factors at play when we work on a family's financial strategy, but I like to think of this as a decent "rule of thumb," so to speak, since age is a very big piece of this.

If you are retired right now and you are, say, in your 70s, you are likely thinking about how much of your pool of assets is on the risk side, and perhaps the adjustment you need to make. But the same should be true if you are in your 20s or 30s. If you are 25 years old, you could be saving for retirement and putting at least 75 percent of your money at risk. Why not take full advantage of the risk/reward factor that the stock market provides? Time, after all, is on your side. Whatever investment strategy you are pursuing, if you just stay the course, you have plenty of time before retirement to recover from and take advantage of any market instability.

Sadly, many young people don't follow the Rule of 100 like they should. Instead of having a healthy amount going into a savings plan, they opt to dump their paychecks on cars, stereos, wide-screen TVs and other expensive toys.

The same lack of fiscal symmetry is true of many retirees as well. I see far too many positioned in a way that much of their savings could be swept away by the next big market crash because far too much of it is at risk.

I have seen the "catch up" syndrome negatively affect the fortunes of many when they are in what I call the "red zone" of retirement... five years on either side. This is when retirees, or those approaching retirement, have a large portion of their savings depleted after a market downturn, and they feel like they must make it up — and fast! In an attempt to do so, they risk more than they should. That might not be such a bad strategy if time was on their side, but it isn't in this instance. They are no longer in their accumulation years. This is a time for them to be cautious with their assets because the next market downturn could catch them by surprise and the risk they took could produce unfavorable rewards, indeed.

CHAPTER 7

Beware of Hidden Fees

"**I** can't understand these things for the life of me," said the 67-year-old woman, gesturing toward a stack of brokerage statements she had just placed on my desk. "I am college-educated, and I was the owner of my own consulting firm before I retired, and I should be able to understand what this stuff means. But it may as well be in Russian."

She is not the only one I hear complain about the cryptic nature of brokerage statements. I must confess that when I began my career as a financial professional, I couldn't make heads or tails of them, either. I can now, of course, but it took some time to learn how to decipher my first one.

"I lost so much money in 2008," said the woman. "How did that happen? I told my agent that I was very, very conservative."

"And what did your broker say to that?" I asked.

"He said he would be conservative in my investments," she said.

After reviewing her statement, it was obvious that her previous financial advisor had either forgotten the conversation with the woman or simply did not have the tools at his disposal to put her in conservative products. The assets in her portfolio were 97 percent at-risk. According to the Rule of 100 discussed in the previous chapter, that may have been appropriate if the woman had been age 3.

One of my office staffers is a whiz at dissecting brokerage statements and breaking out the information so that it can be easily understood. I handed her the statement, and within a few minutes she returned with the statement and a line item explanation of it. Not only did the woman lose money in her account, but she paid the brokerage house handsome fees for the privilege. Understandably, this discovery caused some degree of consternation on her part.

Hidden Fees Are Everywhere

If you want to understand why something happens in the financial world that doesn't seem fair, just follow the money trail. Usually, you will find your answer.

According to a report put out by the Ponemon Institute in 2006, the average American pays just short of $1,000 each year in hidden fees applied surreptitiously by banks, credit card companies, cellular telephone providers, cable and Internet providers, motels and hotels, airlines, grocery stores, and, oh yes, the government.

Banks are notorious for sneaky fees. The newest, and I think the sneakiest, of these fees is when banks quietly impose "maintenance" fees on accounts and implement new charges on mobile phone transactions.

Cellphones are now as ubiquitous as wrist watches. Nearly everyone has one. But researchers estimate most Americans pay approximately $300 per year more than they should for cellphone service. The biggest rip-off is for directory assistance. I thought it was free on mine until I got my bill one month and wondered why it was so high. I was being charged $2 plus airtime. Lesson learned!

The most egregious charge is the early termination of one's contract with the provider. Most of the time, you don't realize this hidden fee until you fall out of love with your cellphone service and try to get a divorce. You either have to wait two years or pay some serious alimony.

Look at your cellphone bill each month. Is it difficult to read? Do you think that may be intentional? According to a 2011 investigation by the Senate Commerce Committee, some cellphone companies have been known to engage in "cramming," that is, allowing a third-party company to attach mystery costs to customers' bills. Investigators report that this has cost consumers at least $2 billion since the 1990s.

Grocery stores are not above fleecing the public, either. If you have that sneaky feeling that you are bagging less but paying more, you aren't dreaming. A watchdog arm of Consumer Reports says corporate food companies have quietly shrunk the quantities of such things as salad dressing, laundry detergent, breakfast cereal, shaving cream, etc. while the prices remain the same. Consumer Reports magazine reported in 2011 that some popular brand ice cream containers that used to hold 16 ounces now hold 14, and dish detergent, which used to come in a 30-ounce bottle, now comes in a 24-ounce container.

Cable companies. Don't get me started! What kills me is that you really don't know what you're paying for. You have to pay for 1,000 channels you don't want just to get the 10 channels you do watch. The same marketing genius who put that together must have invented the same bulk packaging that prevents you from buying just one pocket comb or just one toothbrush.

Have you ever tried to understand your cable bill? It's full of hidden charges for cable boxes, DVR services, surcharges and maintenance fees. You feel helpless because, in most areas, the cable company has a monopoly.

Airlines started charging more for overweight bags, then for extra bags and now they just charge for bags, period. You can get your bags checked "free" if you join the pricy Captain's Club and subscribe to a credit card with a 24 percent interest rate and a $75 annual fee. Even if I am exaggerating a little, I'm not too far off the mark. Nowadays there are fees for rebooking a flight, fees for changing your itinerary and fees for snacks. If you are hungry enough to eat it, a dry turkey sandwich on stale bread can be purchased for around $5. Remember the good old days of free hot meals? Those are long gone. You are fortunate these days if they toss you a pack of peanuts.

I was on a long flight recently, and I decided I would watch the in-flight movie. When I asked the flight attendant for earphones, I was informed that, sure, I could have them… for $5. The flight attendant told me that it would be appreciated if I could come up with the correct change. I just settled for a nap.

I could go on and on here, but you get the picture. Hidden fees are everywhere. And, as much as I hate to be cynical, I believe that when financial companies produce monthly and quarterly statements that are difficult to understand, there might be a reason. There might be something they would prefer we didn't see and didn't ask about.

401(k) Hidden Fees

At this writing, the Department of Labor is requiring 401(k) plan administrators to give employees full details of all the fees they are paying for every $1,000 invested. We will see if this ruling helps matters when these revised statements begin hitting the mailboxes. Hopefully, plan participants will then be able to see just how big of a bite these hidden fees have been taking from their retirement accounts.

When AARP surveyed American workers and asked them if they thought they were paying fees on their 401(k)s, 71 percent of the people surveyed said no. They were shocked to find out that there were record-keeping fees, administration fees and other hidden costs.[4]

Some charges are just downright sneaky. When companies, for example, just allow their 401(k) vendor to pick their funds for them and don't monitor the program closely, it sometimes leads to corruption and under-the-table payoffs. Robyn Credico, senior consultant at the large New York-based human resources consulting firm, Towers Watson, said in an interview with Ross Kenneth Urken of AOL Daily Finance, "sometimes those investment companies say to the record keeper, 'I'll give you a little bit of the investment to offset your record-keeping fees.'"

The big brokerage house that manages the funds, for example, takes a cut from your investment and pays off the record keeper. If your company isn't paying close enough attention, no one notices you are being "cheated" out of your money.

---

[4] AARP. February 2011. "401(k) Participants' Awareness and Understanding of Fees." http://assets.aarp.org/rgcenter/econ/401k-fees-awareness-11.pdf.

Brokerage Account Fees

I saved the best, or perhaps the worst, depending on your frame of reference, for last — brokerage accounts.

Let's say that you inherited $100,000 from someone in your family. You take it to your broker. He says, "What would you like for me to do with this?" and you tell him you would like for him to invest it and make money with it.

So the broker invests the money. Then, 12 days later, you get a statement in the mail. The statement reflects the broker's commission charged by your broker's firm; as a result your balance could be down $5,000 or $6,000. Then you have any underlying costs, in the form of commissions or fees, on each of the products that actually compose your portfolio. If you are invested in mutual funds, you could expect an additional 1-3 percent in underlying costs.

So you call your broker to talk about your newly decreased account value.

"But wait a minute," the broker may say. "Did I mention the fact that the account has an excellent growth potential."

Words such as "potential," "projection" and "prospective" have a way of making me squirm in my chair when it comes to money that people have saved all their lives and are now dependent upon to carry them through their nonworking years. I much prefer words like "contract" and "guarantee."

Maybe your fees are only a few percentage points, but even on an account of $100,000, a few thousand dollars is nothing to sneer at. What if you have a market dip, even just a few percentage points? Those fees can worsen the effect on your portfolio, dragging its value even further down. And when the market rebounds? That's even less money with which to recover your lost assets.

Now, few things in life are free. Any financial product is going to charge something. Whether it's a sales commission or management fee or an assets-under-management fee, you will pay something. But you have the right to know, and to have all the information necessary to question whether you are getting the bang for your buck. It shouldn't require rocket science to be able to calculate whether the money you are paying is reasonable for the services and products you receive.

Here is an excerpt from the United States Securities and Exchange Commission website under the heading, *"Calculating Mutual Fund Fees and Expenses"*:

> *"Fees and expenses are an important consideration in selecting a mutual fund because these charges lower your returns. Many investors find it helpful to compare the fees and expenses of different mutual funds before they invest.*
>
> *"A mutual fund's fees and expenses may be more important than you realize. Advertisements, rankings and ratings often emphasize how well a fund has performed in the past. But studies show that the future is often different. This year's 'number one' fund can easily become next year's below average fund."*

Judith Sheindlin, better known as "Judge Judy," the salty, sarcastic star of a real-life courtroom drama television show, recently wrote a book entitled, *"Don't Pee on My Leg and Tell Me It's Raining: America's Toughest Family Court Judge Speaks Out."* It is aimed at groups in America today who think the rest of us are crazy, stupid or both. I share Judge Judy's sentiment when I analyze statements from financial institutions that slip in hidden fees and conceal unreasonable charges and secret commissions in their fine print and line item entries. It makes me angry. They must think we aren't intelligent enough, or concerned enough, to catch it. The truth is, we are. You are. And more and more Americans are catching on to what they are doing.

CHAPTER 8

Raising a Fist for Senior Power!

Senior citizenship is one of those things that sort of creeps up on you. Life sends you little signals, you know. For example, you never forget the first time it is pointed out to you that you are entitled to senior discounts.

"Do you qualify for our senior discount, sir?" asked the smiling young lady behind the counter at the grocery store. I bristled at first, a bit surprised.

"How old do you have to be?" I asked.

"Sixty." She said.

"Then I suppose I qualify," I admitted.

"You just saved $3.87," she said cheerfully.

I grumbled to myself that I would have gladly paid double than that to not have been so easily spotted and pegged as a "senior citizen." I reasoned that she was so young — she couldn't have been more than 20 years old — that everyone looked ancient to her. The denial continued as I made my way to the parking lot. It was just a fluke. The cashier was just one of those do-gooders that wanted to make sure everyone gets a discount of some kind. She probably offers it to everyone who has the least little wrinkle or a single gray hair.

After denial, however, comes acceptance. I decided to try out my new status at the movie theater. I asked for a senior ticket, and it worked!

"Are you sure you don't want any identification?" I asked the theater ticket seller.

"No, you are fine," said the kid.

Happy about the $2 I had just saved, my swallowed pride went down much easier this time. I even resolved to do some research and see if there were more discounts of which I could take advantage. I was amazed at the list of merchants — many of them right in my backyard — at whose stores I had been paying full price, when there were discounts to be had. It also became obvious to me that, in many cases, if you don't ask, you don't receive.

I checked out a few websites and here is just a sampling of what's out there[5]:

Restaurants

Applebee's®: 15% off with Golden Apple Card (60+)
Arby's®: 10% off (55+)
Ben & Jerry's: 10% off (60+)
Bennigan's®: discount varies by location
Bob's Big Boy®: discount varies by location (60+)
Boston Market™®: 7% off (65+)
Burger King®: 10% off (60+)
Captain D's: discount varies on location (62+)
Chick-fil-A®: 10% off or free small drink or coffee (55+)
Chili's: 10% off (55+)
Cicis®: 10% off (60+)
Culver's®: 10% off (60+)
Dairy Queen: 10% off (60+), varies by location
Denny's: 10% off, 20% off for AARP members (55+)
Einstein Bros.® Bagels: 10% off baker's dozen of bagels (60+)

---

[5] Rebecca Lehmann. Brad's Deals. June 1, 2014. "Senior Discounts: 100+ Stores Offering Discounts for Senior Citizens." https://www.bradsdeals.com/blog/senior-discounts. Last updated Dec. 11, 2015.

Fuddruckers®: 10% off any senior platter (55+)

Gatti's® Pizza: 10% off (60+)

Golden Corral®: 10% off (60+)

IHOP®: 10% off (55+)

Jack in the Box®: up to 20% off (55+)

KFC: free small drink with any meal (55+)

Krispy Kreme Doughnuts®: 10% off (50+)

Long John Silver's®: various discounts at participating locations (55+)

McDonald's®: discounts on coffee every day (55+)

Mrs. Fields®: 10% off at participating locations (60+)

Shoney's®: 10% off

SONIC®: 10% off or free beverage (60+)

Steak 'n Shake®: 10% off every Monday & Tuesday (50+)

SUBWAY®: 10% off (60+)

Sweet Tomatoes®: 10% off (62+)

Taco Bell™: 5% off; free beverages for seniors (65+)

TCBY®: 10% off (55+)

Tea Room Cafe: 10% off (50+)

Village Inn®: 10% off (60+)

Waffle House®: 10% off every Monday (60+)

White Castle®: 10% off (62+)

Retail And Apparel

Banana Republic®: 10% off (50+)

Bealls: 15% off every Tuesday (50+)

Bed Bath & Beyond®: 10% off mailing club (55+)

Belk®: 15% off first Tuesday of every month (55+)

CJ Banks®: 10% off every Wednesday (60+)

Clarks®: 10% off (62+)

dressbarn®: 10% off (55+)

Goodwill®: 10% off one day a week (date varies by location)

Hallmark: 10% off one day a week (date varies by location)

Kohl's®: 15% off (60+)

LensCrafters®: 30% off for AARP members

Michaels®: 10% off on Tuesdays with AARP card

Modell's® Sporting Goods: 10% off

Ross® Stores: 10% off every Tuesday (55+)

The Salvation Army® thrift stores: up to 50% off (55+)

Stein Mart®: 20% off red dot/clearance items first Monday of every month (55+)

T.J. Maxx®: 10% on Tuesdays, varies by location

Walgreens: 15% off on monthly "Senior Day," AARP and 55+ members

Grocery

American Discount Foods: 10% off every Monday (50+)

BI-LO®: 5% every Wednesday (60+)

Compare Foods Supermarket: 10% off every Wednesday (60+)

DeCicco Family Markets: 5% off every Wednesday (60+)

FRESHFARM: 5% off Tuesdays and Thursdays (55+)

Fry's Food and Drug: free Fry's VIP Club Membership and 10% off every Monday (55+)

Great Valu Markets: 5% off every Tuesday (60+)

Gristedes: 10% off every Tuesday (60+)

Harris Teeter Supermarkets: 5% off every Tuesday (60+)

Hy-Vee: 5% off one day a week (date varies by location)

Kroger®: 10% off (date varies by location)

Morton Williams: 5% off every Tuesday (60+)

Pathmark®: 5% off $30 every Tuesday (55+)

The Plant Shed: 10% off every Tuesday (50+)

Publix® Super Markets: 5% off every Wednesday (55+)

Uncle Giuseppe's Marketplace: 5% off (62+)

Travel

Alaska® Airlines: 10% off (65+)

Alamo® Car Rental: up to 25% off for AARP members

American Airlines™: various discounts, call before booking (65+)

Amtrak®: 15% off (62+)

Auto Europe®: 5% off for AARP members

Avis® car rental: up to 25% off for AARP members

Best Western®: 10% off (55+)

Budget® Rental Cars: 10% off; up to 20% off for AARP members (50+)

Cambria® Hotels & Suites: 20-30% off (60+)

Clarion®: 20-30% off (60+)

Comfort Inn®: 20-30% off (60+)

Comfort Suites®: 20-30% off (60+)

Dollar Rent A Car®: 10% off (50+)

Econo Lodge®: 20-30% off (60+)

Enterprise Rent-A-Car®: 5% off for AARP members

Greyhound®: 5% off (62+)

Hampton® Hotels: 10% off if booked 72 hours in advance

Hertz®: up to 25% off for AARP members

Holiday Inn®: 10-30% off depending on location (62+)

Hyatt®: 25-50% off (62+)

InterContinental® Hotels: various discounts at all hotels (65+)

MainStay Suites®: 10% off with Mature Traveler's Discount (50+); 20–30% off (60+)

Marriott℠ hotels: 15% off (62+)

Motel 6™: 10% off (60+)

Myrtle Beach Resort: 10% off (55+)

National® Car Rental: up to 30% off for AARP members

Quality Inn®: 20-30% off (60+)

Red Roof® Inn: 10% off year-round

Rodeway Inn®: 20-30% off (60+)

Sleep Inn®: 20-30% off (60+)

Southwest Airlines®: various discounts, call before booking (65+)

Trailways® Transportation System: various discounts (50+)

United Airlines: various discounts, call before booking (65+)

Activities And Entertainment

AMC® Theatres: up to 30% off (55+)
Bally Total Fitness™: up to $100 off memberships (62+)
Busch Gardens® Tampa Bay: $3 off one-day tickets (50+)
Carmike Cinemas: 35% off (65+)
Cinemark®/Century Theatres: up to 35% off
U.S. National Parks: $10 lifetime pass; 50% off additional services including camping (62+)
Regal Cinemas: 30% off
SeaWorld® Orlando: $3 off one-day tickets (50+)

Cellphone Discounts

AT&T®: Special Senior Nation 200 Plan $29.99/month (65+)
Jitterbug®: $10/month cellphone service (50+)
Verizon Wireless: Verizon Nationwide 65 Plus Plan $29.99/month (65+)

Miscellaneous

Great Clips®: $3 off haircuts (60+)
Supercuts®: $2 off haircuts (60+)

The list is constantly changing, folks, so I invite you to do your own research. Just put the words "senior discounts" into your computer search engine, and you will be amazed. My browser registered 38,800,000 web pages with matching content. I was blown away. Imagine the annual savings if you could discount everything you purchased by an average of 10 percent then take those savings and compound them over time. It would amount to a tidy sum.

Take Advantage of Advantages

During my time as a member of the wrestling team, first at DeKalb High School in my hometown of DeKalb, Illinois, and then at Iowa State University, I learned two valuable lessons:

- When your opponent presents you with an opportunity, take advantage of it.
- Use your advantages to your advantage.

In the world of wrestling, it is rare to have both a size advantage and a speed advantage in each match, but you quite often will have one or the other. If your advantage is size, then use it to win. If your advantage is speed and agility, then use that to win.

Just like those senior citizen discounts we never knew existed, we will discover many more advantages as we approach retirement. These newfound advantages may just replace some of the disadvantages of growing older. I advocate using every advantage that comes our way. After all, we work hard and save diligently so we can enjoy a comfortable life when we retire. Then we may find ourselves grappling with opponents such as inflation, taxes and other expenses we did not anticipate, such as health care costs.

As senior citizens, we may no longer have the physical advantages of youth. We may not be able to run faster than a speeding bullet or leap tall buildings in a single bound. But we do have the special superpowers of wisdom and experience working for us. That should give us a bit of an edge.

These days, older Americans are also imbued with a growing social power. There are 35 million of us now, and more are joining every year. Do you think the local supermarket is offering us a discount just because the owners want to be courteous to old people? Do you think the local movie theater is knocking a couple of bucks off the price of their tickets because they want to show us how sensitive they are? Think again. It is because they, like every other merchant in town, are competing for our dollar. The senior market represents over *$2 trillion* a year. Manufacturers, marketers and merchants know that you are going to be spending your money somewhere. They are well aware that if they fail to compete for your business, you will take it elsewhere.

It is this economic clout possessed by the burgeoning horde of baby boomers that leads me to conclude that, one way or another, and in some form or another, Social Security will continue to exist. Politicians are pandering more and more to the older set. "Gray Power" is the new term for the growing political clout now wielded by older Americans. We are not surprised to hear stump speeches where a candidate positions himself or herself as the stalwart defender of seniors and attacks his or her opponent for threatening Social Security and Medicare. Reform seems inevitable for the Social Security system, but I believe popular demand will keep it alive.

Marketing to Seniors

Gone are the days when marketing to seniors was selling ointments and burial insurance. The Madison Avenue types now know that 70 percent of the buyers of the products they advertise are going to be age 50 or older. Failure to pander to that audience is to lose the best-paying and most loyal consumers there are. Look at it this way. If persons 55 and older control 70 percent of the disposable income in the United States — you can do the math — that means one-third of the nation controls two-thirds of the country's money. Is it any wonder, then, that we are seeing more commercials nowadays featuring people with a little gray in their hair in scenes that depict those people driving sexy sports cars, traveling, living the dream, and not just in commercials selling medicine for aches and pains? Just follow the money trail.[6]

Successful businesses hire experts and consultants to tell them who is the most likely to be interested in and to buy their products and services. Would it surprise you to learn, for instance, that seniors purchase more than one-fourth of the nation's toys? So if you made and sold toys, and you aimed your commercials at only the kids, and left out the grandparents, you would be missing a major segment of your market.

---

[6] Braden Phillips. New York Times. March 4, 2016. "Marketers Take Second Look at Over-50 Consumers."
https://www.nytimes.com/2016/03/06/business/retirementspecial/marketers-take-second-look-at-over-50-consumers.html?_r=0.

We seniors are just beginning to wake up to the degree of influence we have on the world's economy. I also believe corporate America's wave of awareness is just beginning. Hey, by getting my free coffee, dag nab it, I am strengthening the cause of Gray Power!

Senior Computer Literacy

More and more, Grandma is becoming computer savvy. Or, it could be that she was computer savvy all along, and just this last year she became a grandma.

During my interviews with prospective clients, I like to collect as much information as I possibly can so I can better understand their hopes, dreams, aspirations and goals. The conversation inevitably comes around to children and grandchildren.

"Would you like to see some pictures of my grandchildren," said the attractive 62-year-old woman who sat across the desk from me. I was expecting snapshots, but she surprised me by pulling an iPad from her purse and scrolling through the photos of her children and grandchildren.

"Two of them live in California," she said, "so we *Skype* and *Facetime* all the time."

It used to be that older Americans were left in the dust when it came to cellphones and personal computers. No more. Modern retirees are more apt to check on their retirement accounts via a website or a smartphone than they are to wait for their statement to arrive in the mail.

According to one study, the number of Americans age 65 and older who are computer literate rose by 6 million in just five years. What do they do online? According to Pew Research Center, social networking among seniors doubled from 2009 to 2010. Facebook users age 18 to 25 still dominate, numbering over 50 million. But at this writing, the over-

55 age group is approaching 20 million and still growing. Most senior citizens today use a computer and have at least one email address.[7]

The most popular online destination for people over 65 is Google search, which has enhanced the quality of life for older information seekers. What are they looking for? Everything! They look for old friends. They check the weather. They print maps. Those turning 65 use it to cut through the confusing Medicare fog. Like everyone, they surf the Web occasionally just for fun. More and more are paying their bills online, surveys show.

Why would companies be spending billions of dollars to find out what buttons seniors are clicking on their personal computers? Again, just follow the money. These folks have most of the money, and they buy more stuff.

Millions Unclaimed in Discounts

Virtually millions of dollars in senior discounts, as well as government provisions for older Americans, go unclaimed every day. You can't blame restaurants for not advertising the fact that you can save 10–15 percent if you are willing to pay full price. You can't blame the government for burying senior shortcuts and benefits in the small print. But you can blame yourself for not asking. If you want to become more proactive in this regard, the best place to start is on the Internet. Websites promoting senior discounts are springing up like daisies in the spring. Some information is free for the taking. Some sites will charge a reasonable membership fee (less than $15 per year), but once you belong, you can categorize and localize your discount search. Which tire store, for example, located within your ZIP code offers senior citizen discounts? Which garden supply center caters to seniors? SeniorDiscounts.com is a newcomer to the Internet, but as of 2012 it has 40,000 members and provides contact information on more than 150,000 business locations in 50 states that offer discounts to seniors.

---

[7] Pew Research Center. Aug. 27, 2010. "Older Adults and Social Media." http://www.pewinternet.org/2010/08/27/older-adults-and-social-media/.

Joan Rattner Heilman, author of "Unbelievably Good Deals and Great Adventures That You Absolutely Can't Get Unless You're Over 50," says it's "crazy to pay full price for a hotel if you are a senior." Discounts range from 10–50 percent, depending on your age and where you're staying. She gets into public transportation discounts, too.

"There is not a railroad, bus line or public transportation system that doesn't offer a senior discount of some sort," Heilman says, adding that it is important to get the discount when you make your reservation, not when you check in at the station or desk.

"Most times you still have to ask," she says.

Government and Other Programs

Did you know that certain senior homeowners may qualify for a reduction in their property taxes? It's a state-by-state determination and entirely dependent on your state's current tax rules, but it's worth looking into if you are over 65. If you live in Ohio, for example, you can exempt $25,000 of the market value of your home. New York's School Tax Relief Program allows qualifying senior homeowners to exempt $50,000 of their primary residence from school property taxes. You may find more information at your local tax assessor's office.

Health Care Discounts

Would it surprise you to learn that free and reduced-cost prescription drugs are available from sources other than Medicare? One such organization that provides help for seniors is RxAssist (www.rxassist.org), which can help seniors find free or more affordable medications.

The Partnership for Prescription Assistance (www.pparx.org) is a resource that can match seniors with programs that can help pay for medications for those who are eligible.

The Eldercare Locator (www.eldercare.gov) is a free national service of the Administration on Aging in the U.S. Department of Health and Human Services. Since its establishment in 1991, the Eldercare Locator connects those who need assistance on aging with agencies and organizations, both state and local, that render it.

I love the quote by Woodrow Wilson, "I not only use all the brains that I have, but all the brains that I can borrow." One of the ways to color our retirement "green" in these uncertain times is to avoid the tendency to sit in an armchair and complain about rising prices, government cutbacks and higher taxes. Compensate for those negatives by proactively rooting out and taking advantage of every service and provision available to those of us who have earned their badge of honor as a senior citizen.

CHAPTER 9

Take Advantage of the Time Value of Money

To color your retirement "green," you must learn the "time value" of money and use it to your full advantage.

I first came to appreciate that money has a time value when, as a young lad growing up in DeKalb, Illinois, I made extra money during summer months by mowing the lawns of my neighbors. I charged $5 per lawn, and most lawns required me to spend three hours or so mowing, trimming and sweeping the grass off the front sidewalks. Not a bad wage for the early 1960s. They were happy, and I was happy. One day, however, I acquired a new customer, a woman at the end of the block, whose corner lawn was twice the normal size. The grass was high, and the mowing took longer than I had expected. Also, my customer must have misunderstood our simple verbal contract to mean that her $5 entitled her to a lifetime of servitude from this 12-year-old kid. After I had finished mowing, I clipped and swept for another two hours. When I went to tell her that I was finished, and to collect my pay, she would smile sweetly and tell me that there was "just one more little thing" she wanted me to do. Finally, as the sun was fading, she paid me five crumpled $1 bills, the price on which we had agreed. In all fairness, I shouldn't complain. I didn't have the chutzpah to ask for more money, and, looking back, I suppose I did drink a dollar's worth of her lemonade. But it taught me that time equals money and money equals time.

Years later, when I would hear the phrase "time value of money", it would be in a college business course. I would then learn a new dimension of the time value of money. It was basic economics. If I have a sum of money and let someone else hold it for an extended time without charging them interest, I am either a philanthropist or too stupid to handle money. That's why banks charge interest when they lend money. They're not being greedy. Money has a time value.

Also, if you have more than you need for your expenses, it is foolish not to put it to work for you. Over time, unless your money is cultivated and allowed to grow through investments, time will erode its value. A 1950 dollar is now worth $0.04. Most of us don't have a 1950 dollar in our pocket, so what does that really mean?

A Penny Saved

There are four ways we can financially enhance our retirement picture: (1) earning and saving money, (2) properly putting it to work, (3) not losing it and (4) not wasting it.

When Benjamin Franklin came up with his famous maxim, "A penny saved is a penny earned," he was making the point that it does no good to earn money if we turn right around and spend it foolishly. An individual may have a good job, earning an excellent income, but if that person fritters away their income and does not save, then poverty awaits him or her just the same as if he or she had never earned a cent. On the other hand, a person may have a rather modest income, but if he or she is a saver, then good fortune awaits that person just the same as if he or she had earned a great deal of money.

Save, Save, Save

If you are in the accumulation phase of your life, regardless of how much you are earning, make a budget. Living beyond your means is a financial behavioral disorder that afflicts high rollers as well as those of more modest means.

One way to adhere to Ben Franklin's wisdom on saving pennies is to keep a record of your expenses. Full pockets empty the quickest. Plan on how much you will have available to spend on a weekly basis. Take out each week just what you have determined that you can spend and stay on budget with it. I know people who intentionally leave their checkbook, ATM card and credit cards at home so they won't be tempted to use them. Personally, I couldn't do that. Who knows when an emergency might arise? What if the only way to cover it was with your plastic? But I certainly applaud the principle. The point is, be disciplined when it comes to money. If you have cash left over at the end of the week, salt it away in a savings account. If you are saving on a regular basis, then, using the Rule of 100 as a starting point (see Chapter 6), invest it appropriately and regularly and take advantage of dollar cost averaging.

Thrift begins in the brain. When you go shopping, have in mind exactly what you want to buy before you go. If you have a list of things you need, write them down. Check items off the list with **blinders** on.

In rural Illinois, they used to use mules for plowing. These mules would often be outfitted with leather blinders. These flaps were part of the draft animal's harness and were strapped onto the mule's head in such a way as to prevent the animal from being distracted by what appeared in its peripheral vision. Shopping with blinders on can save you a small fortune because it keeps you from buying impulsively. One family, with whom I worked found that, by eliminating impulse buying, they were able to save enough money in one year to pay off all their credit cards and tuck away more than $800 in savings.

When it comes to shopping, make sure you are getting the best deal by comparison shopping. Look for bargains in the local newspaper. Call the stores offering the product and ask if it is on sale. It may be that by waiting a week, you can save money on the purchase. Coupons are a big savings tool if you have the patience to clip them and pay attention to the fine print. But don't buy six cartons of milk to save a dollar. The milk will turn sour.

Groupons are becoming popular with those who are Internet savvy and computer literate. A word of caution, however… put your blinders on here, too. Groupons can dangle things in front of you that you probably don't really need. But if the oil needs changing, and you can buy a Groupon that will do the job for half price, then that's a good deal.

A penny pinched is a penny saved, a penny saved is a penny earned and 100 pennies make a dollar. That may not be as catchy as Ben Franklin's adage, but it is nonetheless true. If you are pinching those pennies, don't just look at the price, look at the value. How much is it per pound, per ounce or per piece. Sometimes you can buy in bulk, but this can be a trap if it forces you to consume more than you really need. You can't always go on price. What if it requires you to drive a considerable distance? You will waste more time and gasoline than the bargain is worth.

When it comes to grocery shopping, store brands, and generic brands if they are just as good, are usually less expensive. Here's a personal testimonial: Don't shop for groceries when you're hungry. Your saliva glands are not connected to your brain.

If you are ever tempted to buy something just because it caught your eye, and you aren't sure if you need it or not, use the 24-hour rule. Remind yourself that you can come back tomorrow and get it if it is something that you really need or want. Most of the time, sleeping on it will erase it from your memory.

We all need entertainment. All work and no play makes Jack and Jill dull people. But you can easily end up dropping $50 at the movies or $100 at a concert in the blink of an eye. Instead, consider going to a high school play or a college concert for free. Rent a movie from one of those $1 boxes you see popping up everywhere. Most libraries have media that you can check out for no charge. Discover reading again. I hear it is actually enjoyable. Free entertainment is everywhere, but it is just like those senior discounts. You have to look for it.

The Rule of 72

When I am called upon to speak on the subject of the time value of money at financial seminars and workshops, I enjoy acquainting the audience with the "Rule of 72." It is great math and great fun. This rule dramatically illustrates the time value of money by showing just how quickly money can grow if conserved and allowed to reproduce. The formula is **72 divided by the interest rate equals the years it takes money to double**. Understanding how this formula works helps us to appreciate the nature of compound interest and how one can build a fortune by putting the concept to work in our personal finances.

- At 6 percent interest, your money takes 12 years (72 divided by 6) to double.
- To double your money in 10 years, just get an interest rate of 7.2 percent (72 divided by 10).

See how it works? You can use the Rule of 72 to calculate other things that double if you know the interest rate. For example, if the country's Gross Domestic Product (GDP) grows at 3 percent per year, then how many years will it take for the nation's economy to double?

Answer — 72 divided by 3, or 24 years.

What if the GDP growth falls to 3 percent? The economy will double in 36 years. If it increases to 4 percent, the economy will double in 18 years.

What else could we use the rule of 72 for? How about inflation?

- If inflation rates go from 2 percent to 3 percent, your money will lose half its value in 24 years instead of 36 years.
- Here's an eye-opener for you. If you pay 15 percent interest on your credit cards, the amount you owe will **double** in only 4.8 years (72 divided by 15).

You can also use the Rule of 72 backward. Let's say you want to double your money in a certain number of years. Divide 72 by the number of years and the result will be the interest rate you need to obtain. Say you want to double your investment in four years (72 divided by 4 = 18). So you need an interest rate of 18 percent. Good luck with that. Let me know how you did it!

To put the rule in more human terms, let's say that you had too much money parked at risk in the stock market when the 2008 crash occurred. Now you have a goal in mind. You need to double your money in seven years to meet it. What rate of return must you earn in order to accomplish this goal?

You would take 72 divided by 7; the answer, 10.2857 percent, is the after-tax amount you need to reach your goal.

Rule of 72 in Income Planning

The Rule of 72 is not lost on those folks in the financial world who structure products and strategies around the income requirements of retirees. One insurance company, for example, marketed an annuity with a guaranteed interest rate on the income account of 7.2 percent. Why that specific rate of return? Because it is easy for the investor to remember that they will double the income account balance in 10 years if they leave the money there and let it earn interest for that length of time.

Insurance companies have gotten a lot smarter in the last few years. When the insurance industry came up with the idea for a fixed index annuity, it was because the traditional fixed annuities just weren't flying off the shelves. In the old days, in order to get a guaranteed lifetime pay-out from an annuity, you had to "annuitize" the contract. That meant you were making a deal with the insurance company that required them to pay you a certain sum of money per month, or per year, for the rest of your life. If you lived a long time, you were the winner. If you died early, the insurance company got to keep what money was left in the account. You can see why those weren't flying off the shelves. The baby boom generation just wasn't going for that deal.

In 2004 or thereabouts, the retirement architects at some of the more forward-thinking insurance companies came up with some revolution-ary ideas that were real game-changers. These new products would:

- Be guaranteed not to lose a penny of the principal due to market loss.

- Credit interest based on the performance of the stock market.
- Lock in any interest and freeze it during market downturns. This feature was called "lock-in and reset."
- Offer a minimum guaranteed interest rate each year.
- Provide for a guaranteed lifetime income *without* requiring that the contract be annuitized, through the use of an optional income rider for which there may be a charge.
- Maintain a reasonable surrender charge period (normally around 10 years).
- Maintain a reasonable surrender penalty for early withdrawal (customarily around 10-12%) that would decline each year until it hit zero.
- Offer options that would include living benefits, such as enhanced death benefits and nursing home benefits.

The name given to this new product at first was "equity indexed annuity." But that was confusing. The public associated equity with home equity. Today these products are better known as "fixed index annuities." They combine the principal protection of the traditional fixed annuity with the potential to earn interest rates based on the growth of the stock market. And you won't experience losses because of the downside of the market, since your money is never actually invested or participating in the market.

How Do They Do That???

Since their introduction, fixed index annuities, or FIAs, have had record growth. According to LIMRA, an independent insurance research organization, sales of FIAs topped $39 billion in 2013, up 16 percent from the previous year.[8] One of the reasons insurance companies can offer such strong retirement products is because they are in the business of "cool risk." Because they use actuaries to identify trends, they

[8] LIMRA. Feb. 24, 2014. "Total Annuity Sales Grow 17 Percent in Fourth Quarter." http://www.limra.com/Posts/PR/News_Releases/LIMRA_Secure_Retirement_Institute _Total_Annuity_Sales_Grow_17_Percent_in_Fourth_Quarter.aspx.

have it figured out how they can offer interest rate guarantees that are considerably higher than those offered by the banking world or the brokerage community.

One high school teacher asked her class of teenage students to write a paragraph on life insurance. What did they think life insurance was? What were their impressions of it? One teenager wrote: "Life insurance is really weird. You really don't get anything for it. It's like, you pay me money now, and then, when you die, I'll pay you money. What's up with that?"

From time to time I talk to the students at one of the local colleges near my home in Elgin, Illinois, about finance. One morning, I was trying to explain to a group of students who had never owned a home how homeowners insurance works. Some of them were incredulous.

"Wait a minute," one said, "You mean I pay $500 a year to the insurance company, and if my house burns down they're going to give me $500,000, or whatever my house is worth? No way, dude."

I had to explain to this skeptical student in terms he could understand.

"Here's how it works," I began. "They've got all these guys they call actuaries. They all carry around their calculators and computers, right? And all they do all day long is study statistics and crunch numbers. They have got it figured out that only four houses out of 1,000 are going to burn down. They tell the insurance company how much they can charge for the insurance policy and still make a profit."

The cartoon bubble that floated above the kid's head still contained a question mark, but I had done the best I could do.

The same principle is true with annuities and income riders that can pay a guaranteed interest rate of upwards of 8 percent on the income account value of a fixed indexed annuity, and still allow the insurance company to make a profit. Actuaries know that some of their policy owners will live to be over 100 years of age, and some of them will die early. It's all about averages and the law of large numbers. To those uninitiated in the ways of insurance companies, these new products sometimes seem too good to be true. Believe me; the insurance companies know what they are doing. They will still make a profit.

Long-Term Care Options

When I do my financial planning seminars, I can get a feel for the ever-changing attitudes and behavior patterns of the participants. I have discovered that few people own long-term care insurance of any kind. There are two reasons for this: (a) We don't like to think about ourselves going into a nursing home and (b) traditional long-term care insurance is a "use it or lose it" proposition.

To have some fun, I like to divide the room into two groups and have one group point to the other group and all say in unison, "You're going to the nursing home, not me." It may sound a bit crazy, but that's how people really think. According to Seniors Site, a Web-based resource for senior citizens, approximately 20–30 percent of all people can expect to spend some time in a nursing home before they die.

I believe a good financial plan is one that anticipates contingencies. Most of us will need long-term care of some kind. LongTermCare.gov estimates that about 70 percent of us will need some type of care, with the average duration of that care at three years. And a quick look at the annual Genworth Cost of Care Survey, which comes out every year and tracks national long-term-care costs, shows that the average national cost of nursing home care is nearing $100,000. One common misconception is that Medicare will cover these expenses. Medicare helps cover up to only 100 days of rehabilitative care. *Medicaid* will help to pay long-term care expenses, but only after the patient has used up his or her own resources and is officially declared a pauper by the state. The quality of care available for those who qualify for Medicaid is limited. With the aging baby boomer generation putting greater demands on a program that is already grossly underfunded, we could expect the quality of care for Medicaid patients to decline even further in the future.

Perhaps the best time to purchase long-term care insurance is when you are young and premiums are relatively small. Many in their 50s and

60s feel long-term care insurance is just too costly. In the unofficial surveys I take at seminars, only one in 10 own traditional long-term care insurance.

Modern Long-Term Care Solutions

Since the "use it or lose it" long-term care policies weren't flying off the shelves, insurance companies had to come up with some alternatives. They, after all, follow the same laws of supply and demand that any other business does. So, once again, the pencil pushers and the slide rule crowd came up with ways to scratch the consumer itch with long-term care options that can be tacked onto annuity and life insurance policies. These options are gaining in popularity because they are much more attractive to the modern consumer.

In one example, an individual buys an annuity with a single premium payment. The product functions exactly like the ones described earlier in this chapter, but there is either a long-term care multiplier built in or there is a long-term care rider available that the owner can purchase. The rules and provisions vary from company to company, some of them requiring a physical, some a health questionnaire and others no underwriting at all. The bottom line is that, in the case of the optional long-term-care rider, the base contract's account value pays for the long-term-care benefit. While this will decrease the contract's account value, it means your long-term care benefit will remain steady for as long as it is in effect.

Another relatively new and innovative approach taken by insurance companies is what is known in the industry as "a combo," short for combination policy. It comes in the form of a fixed annuity. Nothing fancy. Usually it has a guaranteed interest rate, but the other side of the "combo" is long-term care coverage that would pay out two to three times the initial policy value over two or three years after the annuity account value is depleted. For example, a purchaser of a $100,000 annuity who had selected a benefit limit of 300 percent and a two-year long-term care benefit factor would have an additional $200,000 available for long-term care expenses, even after the initial $100,000 annuity policy value was depleted. The policy owner would spend down the $100,000 annuity value over a two-year period and then receive the additional $200,000 over a four-year period or longer. In other words, an annuity purchased with $100,000 could potentially pay out long-term care benefits of $300,000.

One feature that may make these combination annuities attractive is a provision in the Pension Protection Act of 2006 that became effective on Jan. 1, 2010. This provision allows long-term care benefits to be paid from an annuity, tax-free.

These new approaches definitely address a problem, but let me warn you, they are a bit complicated. I recommend that you make an appointment with a financial advisor who is up to date on these new wrinkles and make sure you understand them thoroughly before you purchase one.

CHAPTER 10

The Horrors of Probate and How to Avoid Them

Probate is the legal process of settling a deceased person's estate, which includes paying creditors or debts and distributing the assets of the deceased to the correct beneficiaries.

The term *"probate"* comes from the same Latin word from which the word *probation* is derived. It means "to prove." Often you will hear the phrase, "probate the will," meaning that the wishes of the deceased can't be carried out until the court is satisfied that it is indeed and in truth the decedent's last will and testament and that the terms it contains are indeed and in truth what the deceased wanted to happen. That's why lawyers get involved. It all happens in court before a judge.

The ancient Romans used "oral wills." A Roman citizen who wished to make known how he wanted his affairs handled in the event of his death would "declare his will" in front of seven witnesses. This public statement was regarded as "publishing" his will. The only problem with that was that memories failed and witnesses died. Corruption and greed required that wills be expressed in writing.

The English probate system used religious courts to "prove" or "probate" wills. It wasn't enough for a knight who owned property to declare in writing that his widow should inherit it should he fall in battle. The matter had to be heard before an ecclesiastical judge and "proven" to be true.

The first United States probate court was established in Massachusetts in 1784. It is still a state-by-state arrangement, with procedures and laws as varied as the flag of each state. One commonality, however, is that anyone who dies without a will is considered "intestate," having left no document to testify as to his wishes regarding what he left behind. The court decides who will receive it.

Probate Horrors?

This is all academic until you are the one affected. Then it becomes quite real. Probate horror stories abound, many of them with the same story line. Dad and Mom are killed by a drunk driver, leaving two minor children. Dad and Mom have no will. What happens to the kids? A court will have to step in and appoint a guardian for them without the input of those who knew and loved them. What happens to the assets? A probate proceeding will decide that. What if there are disputes within the family as to who should receive what? It sometimes gets ugly. The kids, after all, are too young to handle money. A conservator is appointed to expend the money for them. Will they have the interests of the children at heart? Let's hope so, but it doesn't always turn out that way.

Consider the case of Anna Nicole Smith, the blonde bombshell who married J. Howard Marshall II, a Texas billionaire 60 years her senior. After the oil baron died, the disposition of his considerable estate landed in a Texas probate court and would be disputed in the legal system for 15 years. While he had showered her with gifts of jewelry, clothing and money, Marshall had never taken any formal action to add Anna Nicole Smith, legally Vickie Lynn Marshall, to his will. The former Playboy bunny died Feb. 8, 2007, from an accidental drug overdose with the case still in dispute.

One of the strangest cases is that of Marilyn Monroe, who died under questionable circumstances in 1962. Her will was probated in New York, and the proceeding was not closed until 2001. When the famous actress died, she was single and childless. After providing $100,000 to care for her mentally ill mother, she left the bulk of her estate to her act-ing coach, Lee Strasburg. Strasburg remarried after Monroe's death. The estate is now in the name of Marilyn Monroe LLC and produces millions of dollars per year for Strasburg's widow, who barely knew Monroe. Experts say Monroe could have avoided the court's 39-year involvement in her estate had she used a revocable living trust instead of a will. Furthermore, she could have specified in that trust that any profits from her ongoing celebrity would be payable to a specific person or a charity.

Probate is Painfully Public

When I left the teaching profession to enter the world of financial planning, I had no idea what probate was. Most people don't know very much about the process.

Before I could "hang my shingle" as a financial professional, I had to take several courses to earn my credentials. It was quite a learning experience. The letters after my name on my business card may look like alphabet soup to you, but they represent hundreds of hours spent in classrooms taking notes and taking tests.

CEP stands for Certified Estate Planner, and it is a designation I earned that means I have a basic knowledge of estate planning. I am not an estate planning attorney, if I had wanted to do estate planning as my job, I would have gone to law school and earned a Juris Doctorate. Instead, I have earned licenses and designations that allow me to work in conjunction with attorneys to make sure my clients have wrap-around services. In addition to a CEP designation, I possess an insurance license and have passed the Series 6, 7, 22, 62, 63 and 65 securities exams and am registered with the state as an Investment Adviser Representative. This way, I can help make estate planning a comprehensive part of my clients' financial strategies, using insurance and investment products and determining how those products can work within an estate plan instead of slapping together products that could cause legal or tax trouble later on.

Truth is, I really didn't strive to obtain so many designations and qualifications because I wanted plaques and certificates to hang on the wall. I have always loved learning. I consider knowledge about the profession I have chosen to be like weapons to a soldier. The more firepower you have at your disposal, the more effective you can be at protecting your position and winning the battle.

I got my most eye-opening education on the ways of probate when I obtained my CEP designation. It's a tough certification to get. Only 2 percent of all financial advisors have it, or so I am told.

As part of my training, I, like the rest of the class, had to go on a bit of a field trip. My instructor told me that I was to go down to the courthouse for the county in which I lived, find the county records department, and walk in and say, "Hello. I would like to see a list of people who have recently died, and I would like to see their original wills."

"This guy's nuts," I said to myself about my instructor. But I followed his instructions. I walked into the Kane County Courthouse in Illinois, and, fully expecting to be thrown out, I announced: "I'm not a judge. I'm not an attorney. I'm here to see people's wills."

"Sure, step right over here," said the woman behind the counter, directing me to a row of computers. I had to sign a form acknowledging that I was not to remove the originals of any document from the room, but I could make copies. That was fine by me.

Imagine that! When I am teaching classes on this at seminars, I will sometimes ask, "Who in the room would like to stand up and tell us all how much money you have and who you want your money to go to when you pass away? While you're at it, give us their complete names, their addresses, their Social Security numbers and their dates of birth."

Naturally, there are no takers.

But there I was, looking over this woman's shoulder at a computer screen. She scrolled down a list of names waiting for me to tell her whose privacy I wanted to invade. I picked a case at random and asked her what some of the numbers mean that appear to the right side of the name of the deceased.

"That's the number of years that the estate has been in probate," she said. The case in question had a little "6" by the name of the departed.

"Does that mean that the estate has been held up in probate for six years, and no one has been paid their inheritance yet?"

"I suppose that's right," she said.

"May I have a few of these files?" I asked.

"You can have all of them if you want," she said.

"I will just take these 15 here," I told her, and she went to retrieve them.

I made an interesting discovery that day. In addition to being blown away by how easy it was to access these private, personal details, I was surprised to see how many of them were still being held up in the probate process. Out of the 15 files she brought me, most of them were relatively small estates. One, however, contained $360,000. It occurred to me how many billable hours could be claimed by attorneys representing both those standing to inherit from the estate and by those contesting it. Six years' worth!

Stop Sibling Squabbles

I grew up with two brothers way before people had automatic dishwashers, at least in my neighborhood, anyway. After every meal, we three boys were to wash, dry and put away the dishes. Every night there was a dispute as to who would do what. If siblings squabble over something as inconsequential as doing the dishes, is it any wonder they might display a contentious spirit over money? Money does crazy things to people... even to people who love each other. When a parent dies and the children are faced with dividing up the possessions, things can get ugly.

So if you don't love your kids, and you want put them in a position where they either have to fight attorneys for something that you intended for them to have, or if you want to cause dissension within your family after you're gone, then just have a will and nothing else. That is a sure way to have your estate go to probate. But if you want to prevent all that hassle, get with an estate planning attorney and see if you might benefit from having a trust drawn up.

When I began my career as a financial advisor, I had the mistaken impression that trusts were invented by the Kennedys and the Rockefellers. I learned otherwise. You may find it useful to have a trust if:

- You have a sizable portion of your assets in real estate or a business.
- You want to leave your assets to heirs in such a way that it is not immediately payable to them. You may wish to leave it to a child, for example, in lump sums when they achieve goals or reach life landmarks, such as graduating from college, etc.
- You have a complex family situation that requires adjusted timelines. You want to care for your spouse first, for instance, but if he or she should die, you wish the remainder to go to your children from a previous marriage.
- You have an heir who is disabled, and you want to provide for him or her without interfering with some type of government assistance.

Trusts are useful estate-planning tools for many other situations, such as reducing estate and gift taxes, but the main advantage they provide is that they put specific conditions on how and when your assets are to be distributed after your death, and they distribute assets to heirs efficiently without the needless publicity, cost and delay of probate. The cost of a basic trust plan can be anywhere from $1,500 to $3,000, and maybe more, depending on the complexity of the trust. But since probate can chew up 5-7 percent of your estate, it makes the cost of seeing an estate attorney to have one drawn up seem negligible indeed.

Designated Beneficiaries Avoid Probate

Another way to avoid the evils of probate is to arrange your affairs in such a way that you use financial instruments with designated beneficiary stipulations, such as IRAs, annuities and life insurance.

When I do my three-step review with new clients, one of the first things I look at on all documents is the beneficiary page, if there is one. It often needs updating. The reason this is so important is because the beneficiary designation is incontestable. The name listed on the line will be the person to whom the money goes, regardless of any logic or circumstances that present themselves after the fact. In one instance, a man left his ex-wife as the sole beneficiary of a life insurance policy after he remarried. Upon his death, his widow was disenfranchised while his ex-wife, who had remarried, received the proceeds from the policy.

Living Wills and POAs

Frank and Mary are on a trip. They have a terrible car accident. The good news is they aren't killed. The bad news is they are hospitalized for seven or eight months. Who is going to make sure the utility bills are paid so the pipes don't freeze? Who is going to be able to step into their lives and act on their behalf? It will be whoever has the long-term *power of attorney*. Is that a document that you have on file with your estate planner or attorney, with a copy in a fireproof safe at home?

We have all heard the horror stories that result from the absence of a *living will.* The most widely known is perhaps the case of Terri Schiavo. She collapsed at her home in St. Petersburg, Florida, in 1990, and remained in a vegetative state for the next eight years. Kept alive by machines, but with no apparent hope of ever regaining awareness, her husband finally decided have the feeding tube removed, which would end her life. The parents fought the move, and the case dragged on in the courts until 2005, while a nation wondered, "What would Terri have wanted?" A living will would have settled the issue quickly.

Legal Review

When it comes to estate planning, every estate is different. There is no easy, one-size-fits-all matrix to use and, regardless of what you may hear, there is no fill-in-the-blank form that you can use that will stand up to the scrutiny of the American legal system. That's why I recommend that you sit down for a consultation with a competent, qualified estate planner and allow him or her to review all of your documents completely to determine what needs to be updated, amended, added or deleted. In many cases, such initial consultation sessions are done without charge.

Once the proper legal documents are in place, I suggest they be reviewed every three years. Many documents are state specific. Life happens. People move. Laws change. People die. People are born. Usually, once these documents are in place, such minor changes are done without charge.

CHAPTER 11

Income Buckets That Never Run Out of Money

Regardless of what your job is and what it requires of you, to find true happiness and satisfaction in your work you must find the more noble reason for what you do.

For example, there is the story about a man who walks up to a construction site and asks three workers in succession what they are doing.

"What does it look like?" says the first worker. "I'm laying bricks!"

The man walks up to the second worker and asks him how he is doing.

"I guess I'm doing OK," he replied. "I'm just working hard, laying some bricks, trying to make a living."

He approaches the third worker and says, "I guess you're just like the other two guys, just working hard, laying bricks, eh?"

"Oh no, I'm not just laying bricks, I am building a church," said the worker with a big smile. "Right about here is where the steeple will eventually go. People will be bringing their families here to this building to worship together for hundreds of years after I'm long gone."

Sometimes when people ask me what I do for a living, the short answer — financial advisor— just doesn't seem to express it. I would rather tell them, "I help take the worry and fear out of retirement by establishing a lifetime income strategy for my clients." I can't help it if that sounds a bit sappy. It is just more my view of what I do. One client with whom I had worked for a number of years corrected me when I told him that I used to be a teacher.

"You're still a teacher," he told me. "You just teach people what to do with their money."

The Case of Jim and Jerry

I'd like to tell you about the situation of two brothers I know. Perhaps you can relate. Let's call them Jim and Jerry. It had been a tough year for both brothers with the recent death of their 92-year-old mother. Jerry was at Jim's home. They were sitting at the table, having a cup of coffee, and talking over some of the family matters that they had to care for with their mother's passing, when Jerry noticed that Jim had a stack of unopened mail. There were at least six or eight envelopes there, all from "Smith Barney," a large brokerage firm. Concerned, Jerry asked Jim about the unopened mail.

"What's this?" asked Jerry, gesturing to the stack of envelopes.

"It's all bad news," Jim replied. "I don't want to open it."

"That settles it," Jerry said. "You need to see someone."

Of course, that's the point where Jim decided to involve a financial professional. I might be biased, after all, my firm specializes in working with folks in or near retirement, but I'd say Jim's decision to seek help was wise.

Jim's Troubles

I said Jim and Jerry had a hard year, didn't I? Well, this was especially true in Jim's case. He had lost his wife about a year and a half ago. He felt like his financial life was in disarray. With the settlement of his mother's estate, Jim had around $250,000 on which to live the rest of his retired life.

Jim carried a small notebook in his pocket, on which he kept track of his needs, wishes and troubles. In his notebook were four struggles.

No. 1: When his wife died, the family no longer had income from her Social Security check. Jim wanted to be able to make about $941 a month to maintain his lifestyle.

(According to Social Security rules, when a spouse dies, his or her Social Security income stops. If you are the surviving spouse, you get to keep either your Social Security benefits or half of your spouse's, whichever is higher, so this was a pretty typical scenario.)

No. 2: Because Jim was not acquainted with the Rule of 100 (see Chapter 6) or an equivalent rule of thumb, he hadn't realized that he was taking on more market risk than is necessary or good at his age. He had experienced losses as a result and felt powerless to prevent them. All of this accounted for the unopened envelopes on his table. His second goal was to protect a portion of his assets. He never wanted to be afraid of opening another financial statement again.

No. 3: Understandably, as Jim anticipated a long life, he wanted to know his assets had some room to grow to account for inflation and other needs.

No. 4: Before his wife died, Jim's daughter had a baby. His wife was alive long enough to be able to see their granddaughter, but had died three months after the baby had been born. Within six months of his wife's death, as Jim says, his son-in-law turned into an "outlaw," leaving Jim's daughter and granddaughter to fend for themselves. No. 4 on Jim's list was to prepare his assets in such a way that they could benefit his daughter and granddaughter as much as possible when he was no longer there to protect them.

I know of many people who are in situations like this. In fact, I see these scenarios in my office more than I care to admit. That's why I try to make it a point to listen more than I talk, especially during first interviews. As my mother used to say, "God gave us one mouth and two ears for a reason; we should listen twice as much as we speak." In my practice, I find that this is particularly important for all of my clients.

Buckets of Money

It is always a pleasure to work with someone who has easily definable goals. Whatever plan we devise for a person's assets, knowing each person's goals and aims is central; if a plan doesn't fit those goals, then it isn't the plan for them.

Yet, each plan may have some commonalities. For instance, for someone like Jim, who is close to or in retirement, we will almost certainly begin by assessing how much risk their portfolio has, and whether it is reflective of their point in life. Often, I find people are overexposed. From there, we rebalance a portfolio to be more in line with their risk tolerance and goals.

While everyone's circumstances will dictate a different approach, one of our oft-used strategies is to take the money we have designated for conservative strategies and use it to create four buckets of money, each designed to perform a separate task. This is not a particularly new strategy. It goes by different handles. Some call it the "tiered income system," or "bucket system." In any case, here is how it might work. Using, say, $250,000, we can create the following sources of income for a 20-year span, at least:

Bucket One — $45,000. This bucket will produce a steady and reliable income of $1,000 per month for the next five years, perhaps using an annuity contract that can continue to earn interest while it pays out.

Bucket Two — $45,000. This bucket is the second "tier." For the five years that Bucket One is active, we will allow any annuities here to grow. This will also give any investments we use here some time to hopefully realize some solid market gains, depending on market fluctuations. After Bucket One has paid all its money out, we will look to this bucket to pay out the $1,000 per month for another five years.

Bucket Three — $35,000. This bucket's assets are positioned to grow, untouched, for 10 years while Buckets One and Two are doing their jobs. Beginning in year 10, this bucket will pay out $1,000 per month.

Bucket Four — $125,000. This bucket may be a mix of life insurance products, like annuities, and investments. Using bells and whistles such as riders, plus 15 years of untouched growth potential, we can expect this bucket to produce $1,000 of guaranteed income for the rest of a person's life, plus contingencies for inflation. Depending on how long this person lives, we may also have enough left over to work into a legacy.

Add up what the buckets contain, and you will get $250,000. It's what we do with the money that creates the "magic." We use the money's time value for return potential and interest growth for the later buckets while at the same time providing income guarantees and making sure that whatever is left in the buckets, after they have finished paying and growing, is left to heirs.

Now, of course this example is hypothetical—just an example of one strategy we commonly use. A strategy like this may not make you a gigagillionaire, and my example here isn't a universally applicable strategy. For instance, it doesn't include the possible assets you would want to have outside of your income products — having a certain amount of liquid cash for emergencies, for example. But it can certainly make sure someone has a cash flow without massive tax liabilities, a cash flow on which they can depend for personal income to pay the bills and sustain their lifestyle. When it comes to the strategy, products or advice that we give, we of course tailor everything to the needs and goals of each individual, which is why it's important to work with a financial professional who can do just that.

Exclusion Ratio

One of the most favorable elements in a strategy such as our tiered buckets, which utilize fixed annuities, is the exclusion ratio. Any time income is received from an annuity, it is possible that a portion of the income payout is exempt from current income tax, since it was likely taxed upfront. The way we structured the payout on the $1,000 per month in the previous bucket example, we could expect to see 97 percent, or, in this case, $970 of the $1,000 monthly payment, be exempt from additional taxation. According to IRS rules, and because of the vehicles we frequently use for a strategy like this, the payments mostly represent a payback of initial premium instead of capital gains, according to the Internal Revenue Code.

Flexibility

Every situation is different. Because we design our own plans around our unique circumstances, wishes, goals and dreams, we are able look at a sample plan and say, "I would like for this bucket to grow for 15 years. Show me what difference that would make in my payout."

Or, in the interest of having more cash at our disposal, we could say, "Show me what this would look like if we let it grow for five years... or eight years." Through the magic of computers, we can adjust the figures and guarantee (not just project) certain outcomes through using insurance products that can affect retirement income dramatically.

Don't Kill the Golden Goose

Anyone who knows me knows I am passionate about financial protections for seniors. Nothing irks me more than to see the grief and pain that some so-called financial professionals bring upon retirees, or those approaching retirement, by playing fast and loose with their money. There may be exceptions to the Rule of 100, and there may be a little wiggle room in the conservative/growth-positioned asset ratio, but the exceptions are few, and the wiggle room is minimal.

With the right planning, the same people who were once afraid to open account statements can find confidence and comfort in knowing, sometimes to the dollar, how much income to expect each month for as long as they live. That is hard to put a price on these days.

When Babs and I were in the child-rearing mode in DeKalb, Illinois, we used to read to our kids, Blakely, Kylee and Trace, each night at bedtime. One of the children's favorite stories was "The Goose That Laid the Golden Eggs." Looking back, I suppose the moral of that story was if you have a goose that is providing you with golden eggs, you don't want to kill that goose. In fact, you need to keep that goose protected and safe from all harm.

What happens if you wake up one day and you have no more money? How many wish to saddle up and go back to work in our 70s?

In the case of Jim, some of his nest egg was in the form of an IRA. He wanted to be sure he could pass on whatever was left in it, so he positioned it so it could be multigenerational. Jim should live a good, long life. His parents lived to be 92 and 91. But, if all goes well for him in retirement, a competent financial advisor should use estate planning strategies to help him in his goal of preserving enough money to make a difference in helping his kids and grandkids. Some of it will be taxable and some of it won't. Hopefully, Jim will position his IRA and other assets in a way that as little as possible will be lost to the taxman, and as much as possible will go to Jim and then to his family.

CHAPTER 12

Five Ways to Color Your Retirement Green

I promised you five ways to color your retirement green, and they are here in this chapter. Thank you for reading this far.

If I have learned anything about solving financial problems in the last three decades, it is that there is no such thing as an easy solution to anything. When it comes to financial planning, there is no one-size-fits-all remedy to complex and individual money ailments. We are all unique individuals with our own goals, tolerances, wishes, hopes and dreams.

But just as there are fundamentals to physical health, such as eat right, get plenty of exercise and don't smoke, there are certain basics to fiscal health as well, and you will suffer if you ignore them. Preventive medicine is the best kind to take. Steps taken as a precaution in financial matters can be just as important. Much of the advice I am called upon to give when counseling clients falls into the category of problem-solving and is not preventive in nature. This is not unusual. Most people don't visit the doctor until something hurts or doesn't work like it should. It is the same with our money affairs. We often don't seek the help of a financial professional unless there is a problem.

I have had seminars on financial planning and money management that are packed after notable financial turbulence, like a Wall Street crash. There is wall-to-wall worry and concern, and people are looking for answers. Many of them have seen their savings diminished by unexpected events. Their financial house, now in disorder, is in need of repair. Just as it is impossible to unring a bell, it is impossible to undo the damage that might be done by such financial cataclysms. What is possible, however, is to begin taking steps from that moment on that will prevent exposure to future danger.

Paradigm Shift

Some of the measures I will advocate here are remedial in nature. That is, they may require you to re-think things a bit. The buzzword for that type of mental exercise is "paradigm shift." A paradigm is a pattern of thought. A shift, then, would be a change in that pattern of thought. This is not an easy thing to do. It seems to be against human nature to change. We like things comfortable and customary in our lives. If you don't believe me, try parting your hair on the other side for a change. Or try sleeping on the other side of the bed one night. Do you put on your right shoe first and then your left? Try reversing the process. It's hard to do, isn't it? We resist change like we shield our eyes from sudden bright light. We don't like new patterns in most anything that has become routine. But change happens whether we want it to or not. The few who welcome change to their worlds with open arms and don't mind shifting their paradigms to accommodate it, especially if it is beneficial change, are usually more successful. They turn the unexpected into an opportunity for growth.

As I have often mentioned in this book, I work mainly with older Americans, those who are either retired or on the verge of retirement. This resistance to change is especially pronounced in our age group. Change produces fear… Fear of the unknown. What conquers this fear is knowledge — turning the unknown into the known. That is why I am such an enthusiastic proponent of education in the area of financial matters. The more you know about your money, where you have it and why you have it there, the more confident you become about your financial future. The more knowledge you accumulate about the financial strategies that are available to you, the less likely you will be to make poor decisions that could endanger your financial future. Fear is an affliction of the uneducated. Adapting to change will never be easy, but it will be possible if we know the field on which we are playing.

Coloring It Green

I was on a family vacation cruise to the southern Caribbean a few years ago and, prior to going ashore on an island just north of Venezuela, I had to see the purser and exchange some of my United States currency for a few Bolivars, the currency for the Isla De Margarita. I was immediately struck by how colorful their money was. Our American $1 bill looked downright anemic by comparison. Even the line-cut images of our founding father, George Washington, with his placid, somewhat mild-mannered expression, seemed lackluster compared to the Technicolor visage of Simon Bolivar with his fierce stare and piercing, dark eyes. Bolivar was the 19th century independence hero who founded their country, and whose portrait now takes up considerable space on their currency. After someone explained to me that one of our dollars was worth four times as much as one Bolivar, I was much more content with the muted green and gray of our bucks. After a little drive through the countryside of this little island, I was shocked to see the poverty of its people. Greenbacks are just fine with me.

Why is our money green? No one really knows for sure, but a common explanation is that it was the color of ink that was readily available and in large supply when large amounts of paper money began appearing during the Civil War. It was kept when the size of bills became smaller in 1929 because the ink was strong and it didn't rub off as easily as some other inks the government tried. This was seen as a good thing since the bills would receive much handling.

What makes the ink appear green is actually a carefully produced mixture of several different color inks, a recipe that is kept secret to prevent counterfeiting. In recent years, we have seen more color appear in larger American bills, but green is still the dominant color, mainly because of tradition. Besides, if we change the dominant color to, let's say, red, we would then have to change our nickname for the U.S. dollar from "greenback" to "redback." I'm sorry, but that just wouldn't be right.

Coloring your *retirement* green means just what it says… coloring that "no work" zone green with money so you won't run out of the stuff just when you need it the most, which, by the way, is an occurrence that people say they fear more than heights, snakes, spiders and public speaking. Here are the five ways to color your retirement green.

#1 Live Within Your Means

Were you looking for something sexier and more profound? I'm sorry. This may seem like basic stuff, but the words, "Live within your means" are perhaps the four biggest words in the English language when it comes to fiscal health, and for some it is way easier said than done.

Along with the obvious advantages that come from living in a progressive economy and a cornucopian society such as ours, there is also the curse of wanting it all and not being able to afford it. There are homes, cars, boats, trips, jewelry, fine dining and much more to be had, and it is all at our fingertips waiting for us to reach out and take it. If you judge by the endless commercials on television, we deserve it all, too. The reality, of course, is that, for most of us, anyway, it is beyond our reach. We can't afford it. But wait! We can get it now and pay for it later!

I remember as a teenager seeing a credit card for the first time. It was called "Master Charge" and it had just come out. The credit card was an extension of the old revolving charge programs started by large department stores, like J.C. Penney and Macy's to replace the "lay-away plan." Why lay it away and make payments on the item until you had paid for it in full, and then take it home, if you could have the immediate gratification of taking the item home and paying for it in installments? With the new credit cards, you could purchase virtually anything, virtually anywhere, with plastic.

Years later, Master Charge became MasterCard and would soon be joined by Visa, American Express, Discover and others. "Buy now — pay later" became the mantra of every advertising pitch. Anything you wanted was now "affordable at low monthly payments."

Here's a major truth, America: You can't even begin to save for retirement if you are mired in credit card debt. Consumer credit debt is a poison that prevents many of its victims from living the carefree retired life they may have dreamed of during their working years. Debt is the antithesis of financial success. It is the minus column on the balance sheet that must be accounted for before anything positive can begin.

How many people in America live beyond their means? According to NerdWallet's "2016 American Household Credit Card Debt Study," the total U.S. consumer debt was $12.58 trillion. While the major share of this is mortgages, student loans and auto loans, credit cards represent $779 billion. This kind of debt is the worst kind. It represents high-interest debt not backed by collateral, such as a house or a car. These loans are signature loans. They are tabs allowed by banks on the basis of your credit score. The average annual percentage rate (APR) of interest on these credit cards is 18.76 percent, according to the report. The average credit card debt, for those families who carry it, is $16,748.

The baby boom generation is no stranger to consumer credit debt. We grew up with it. How are members of the boom generation coping with it, now that they are approaching retirement? Not too well.

According to Sean Bryant, who collected several data points for his Investopedia article, "Why Retirees Are Carrying More Debt Than Ever," the average credit card debt for Americans 65 to 69 is $6,876, with those 75 and up holding $5,638. In fact, since 2013, more than 65% of households headed by those 55 and older carry debt. Here's a startling statistic: bankruptcies declared by people 55 and older tripled from 1991 to 2007, and have continued to climb, accounting for nearly a quarter of all cases nationally.[9]

According to the U.S. Bureau of Economic Analysis, between 1993 and 2008, personal savings rates in America hit their lowest levels since

---

[9] Mark T. Young & Associates. Feb. 14, 2013. "Bankruptcy among older Americans is growing." http://www.marktyoung.com/blog/2013/02/bankruptcy-among-older-americans-is-growing.shtml .

the Great Depression of the 1930s. Then they rose steeply in 2009 to 6.9 percent, and have since leveled out, usually between 5 and 6 percent of a person's take-home pay, with 2016 ending at 5.6 percent. What happened? When a recession hits, like the one that followed the market crash of 2008, it usually comes on the heels of a borrowing binge. The great "debt bubble" that caused the Great Recession of 2008 was the jolt Americans needed to get them to wake up and smell the coffee. Warning! Warning! Debt can be dangerous to your wealth! If there was one bright spot to the housing crisis and the economic disaster that followed, it was that Americans finally began to sense their own fiscal mortality and realize that if they didn't end the binge, they would be soon be over the edge and off the cliff. As a whole, Americans stopped their binge spending. Some didn't stop soon enough, however. Bankruptcies nearly doubled by the end of 2009, according to the National Bankruptcy Research Center.[10]

Debt holds such a central part of American spending that we have reality TV dedicated to it, like one program on CNBC entitled "Til Debt Do Us Part." It is a reality show where couples allow cameras to invade their financial lives, allowing for a voyeuristic peek at what credit abuse does to families. As the title suggests, these are people who can't stop shopping, and now their money problems are tearing at the fabric of their lives. The host of the show, Gail Vaz-Oxlade, takes a tough-love approach to helping these couples extricate themselves from the debt web and get on the road to financial recovery. In the one episode I watched, the couple was in their late 30s. He earned $60,000 per year and she earned $50,000 per year. They lived in a nicely appointed, well-furnished townhouse, they owned two cars, they had several high-definition televisions and all the other electronic gadgetry associated with modern life. After taxes, their combined net income was $6,000 per month. They were spending $7,500 per month. Do we see a problem developing here?

---

[10] National Bankruptcy Research Center. November 2009. "National Bankruptcy Research Center November 2009 Bankruptcy Filings Report." https://www.nbkrc.com/November2009_News.aspx.

The camera crew followed the wife as she shopped for a new luxury car, a Mercedes. We listened as she discussed the purchase with the salesman. I felt relieved when she left the showroom without buying it. Then it was the husband's turn. His weakness was electronic gadgets. We watched helplessly as he purchased more gizmos to add to his collection. At home, they squabbled over money, each accusing the other of being out of control.

In the next scene, however, it was time for the tough love administered by the show's host. She put them on a strict budget. No more shopping sprees. They agreed to pay $2,000 per month toward their credit card debt until they were debt-free. One of the more amusing scenes took place when the couple was forced to realize that their entertainment budget was only $40 per month. They had to discover such forgotten pastimes as fishing and hiking for family diversion.

Happily, the result was a mended marital rift and a renewed understanding of how toxic consumer debt can be. According to Vaz-Oxlade, 90 percent of all divorces are because of disagreements over money.

You May Be a Spendthrift If

As Jeff Foxworthy would say, "You may be living beyond your means if..."

- **Your credit score is below 600.** Credit bureaus keep track of all kinds of things that go to make up a credit score, which in turn reflects your credit worthiness. Scores range from a low of 300 to a high of 850. It is this score that lenders use to determine if they will lend money to you. If your score is under 600, you are probably in over your head.

- **You are saving less than 5 percent** of your income. If you are in your accumulation years nearing retirement, this is a minimum. Ten percent would be better. If you want financial security during your golden years, you simply cannot be neglecting this. And that's 5 percent of your gross income you should at least be saving, not net.

- **Your credit card balances are rising.** This is an obvious one, but the importance of paying down credit card balances as soon as possible can't be overstated. The trick is to pay off your credit card bills as soon as you receive them and purchase only what you know you have the cash to pay for. I know. It's easier said than done. But making the minimum payment on credit cards and carrying a balance pushes a "green" retirement further and further away. If you have $5,000 in credit card debt, and you make the minimum payment of, say $200 per month, toward it, it will take you 13 years to pay it off and you will end up paying almost double the amount you originally owed.

- **More than 30 percent of your income goes to your house.** Add up your mortgage payment, property taxes and insurance. If it's more than 30 percent of your gross income, then you are living beyond your means, according to most experts. Is it possible to downsize? If you can downsize, is it possible to put any equity toward your retirement savings program? Is it also possible to do the same with the extra money you are now not spending on housing? You may be surprised how much impact compound interest over time will have on your retirement picture if this is possible.

- **You have overdue bills.** A good rule of thumb is that, if you are fiscally healthy, you pay your bills, in full, as soon as they arrive, and you are done with them. But buying on credit and paying by installment has become a national illness. What's an extra $40 per month, right? But soon, all those bills start to pile up. You rob Peter to pay Paul, and your monthly income is spread thinner and thinner. If that sounds familiar, try this: spread all of your monthly bills out on a desk, or table. Go through them one by one. See which ones you can eliminate, if it is a service, or pay off if it is a debt. Do you really need all those premium channels? Is it really necessary that your cellphone have the capability of detecting a nuclear strike? Just like a captain will lighten the load to save a sinking ship, you must ditch the things you can do without. You may be surprised at how much you can save. Don't forget to put the savings toward first paying off all consumer debt and then toward your retirement

#2 Keep Your Savings Protected

Again, I'm sorry to disappoint if you anticipated some sage stock market tip that would make you an instant millionaire. No, I'm afraid I don't know what the next Google is. I can't tell you what the price of oil will be next year this time. What I can tell you is that if anyone claims to have such knowledge, run away if they are giving you financial advice. They don't know either.

I can also tell you that you don't need this type of information to color your retirement green. What you do need is to have the simple concept of conservative money investing on your side.

Do No Harm

Do doctors still take the Hippocratic Oath? I have a couple of friends who are doctors, and I asked them about it. Neither of them remembered taking it nor did they remember what the oath said. Have you ever read it? It involves swearing to the god Apollo and several other mythical deities, that, as a physician, you will do this or that, or not do this or that. In one place, the doctor vows not to "use the knife" on a patient. Does that mean surgery? I think it does.

There is one part of the oath I like very much. It's the part where the doc promises to "do harm to no one." In other words, you may not be able to heal the patient, doctor, but you are promising that you will at least do the patient no harm. I bring this up because I think financial advisors should be required to take a similar oath before they can hang out their shingle. They need to promise, in whatever flowery language that would make it binding and official, that they would never give any client advice that would go against a client's best interest, no matter what the advisor's benefit might be.

I have seen too many long faces on individuals who had saved their entire lives, doing without extravagant vacations and living modest life-styles, so they could preserve a nest egg for their retirement years, only to see a market reversal back over it like a bulldozer tread and crush it lifeless. Where was their financial advisor? How did he allow this to happen? What advice did he or she have for them after the crash? Was it to drink more of the Kool-Aid? Just hang in there, and it will all come back?

I have concluded that most of those in the financial community who would put the life savings of seniors at risk in a volatile market do so not because they are malicious or greedy, but because they simply don't know any better. They are uneducated in conservative strategies. I choose to believe this because to subscribe to the alternative would be to assume that these guides purposely advise their charges to walk into are-as that are unsafe. I have too much faith in the goodness of human na-ture to believe that.

I am convinced they mean well, but they are like the carpenter who goes to work with only one tool... a hammer. And like the old proverb says: "To someone one whose only tool is a hammer, every problem looks like a nail."

To keep your savings protected, you first need to understand how the Rule of 100 guideline applies to you when it comes to investing. If you need to review that, it's back in Chapter 6.

Competent financial advisors who keep up with modern investment trends and cutting-edge retirement products will know how to position your assets in such a way that an appropriate portion of your assets have guarantees, not just projections. Your options are not limited to sluggish returns that cannot outpace inflation, either.

When I was a young man, still teaching, I received a sum of cash from an inheritance. It wasn't a large amount of money — a little over $3,000 — but it was a lot to Babs and me at the time. We were current on our bills, and I knew the prudent thing to do was to save the money. I asked a good friend, and the advice I received was that if I wanted a good return on the money, I should take the check to a large brokerage firm and let them tell me how the money should be invested.

The firm was housed in an impressive building, and the people were friendly. I was asked to wait for a few minutes, and then escorted over to a cubicle where I sat across from a very pleasant young man at a glass desk. I told him that I would like to invest the cash, and he reached into a drawer and withdrew what looked like a brochure illustrating three choices in the form of a circle with different colored wedges.

Choice No. 1 was for ultra-conservative investors. The pie sections for money market funds were fat, and the pie sections for market investments, such as small cap stocks, large cap stocks, mutual funds and international stocks were skinny.

"Don't expect much in the way of a return from this one," he told me, "the more conservative you are, the less return you get."

Choice No. 2 was for folks in the middle. The mutual fund pie sections were wider in this one. So were the pie pieces that represented stocks.

"This is the one most people go with," he said. "It's the most balanced."

Choice No. 3 was nearly all mutual funds, small and large cap stocks, a hefty slice of international stocks and a big chunk of growth stock funds.

I took Choice No. 2. What did I know? It was the most popular. I honestly don't know what happened to that money. It was later moved into an IRA and has since become part of the larger picture of our retirement savings. But I don't think the business of "investment counseling," as I was exposed to it that day, has changed much. I call it the cookie-cutter approach. "Here are three formulas. Which one do you want? A, B or C?" The conservative option gets you such minimal returns that I think it is tantamount to putting your money in a Mason jar and burying it in the backyard. Middle isn't much better. Your money is put where the prospect of loss is minimized, but returns are unpredictable at worst and predictably low at best. Choice No. 3 is Las Vegas revisited.

Years later, when I began studying for my certification as a financial planner, I would think back about my visit to that large brokerage house. Granted, it wasn't a large amount of money, but I got the feeling that I would have been treated the same as if I had walked in with a $100,000 check. The same desk drawer would have opened. I would have been handed the same slick-paper brochure with the same three circles staring up at me, waiting for me to choose one of the three pies. During my first year as a financial professional, I realized that my first obligation as an advisor was to know what I was doing. I vowed never to come across to my clients like that smiling but uninformed young man behind the glass desk in the cubicle at the big brokerage house. It may not matter so much if you are dealing with a month's pay, but when a life's savings is on the line, it matters a great deal.

"How much of this amount are you willing to lose," is one of my favorite questions to ask those contemplating rolling over funds from a large brokerage house to a less risky account. Invariably the answer comes back, "None of it!"

"Good answer," I will tell them. And, for most of them, it is a good answer. Let's build on that.

#3 Put Your Money to Work for You

I actually know some people who have buried money and gold in their back yard. They are not kooks, or even what you would call eccentric in other respects. They have just lost faith in the banks and the financial system and have taken a portion of their liquid assets and hid them where only they know where to find them.

Do you have substantial amounts of money parked in money market funds? With interest rates the way they are at the time of this writing, that's about the same as putting it under the mattress. Don't get me wrong, I am not against keeping an emergency fund for unexpected expenses. That is part of a good financial plan. Emergency money needs to be extremely liquid. I mean the kind you can access from an ATM or a check or debit card. I understand, also, that there are places you may wish to park money for short-term goals, like a down payment on a new car or home. But aside from that, your assets need to be working for you if you want a green retirement.

People sometimes confuse **conservative** money with **unproductive** money. Nothing could be further from the truth. Strategies are available in the modern world of investing that will allow you to trade time for money.

Think of yourself as the boss and think of your money as your employee. Do you really want to see your money standing around idle, like those office employees who seem to huddle around the water cooler? That won't make your "business" thrive. Parking your money in a certificate of deposit, a money market fund or some other place is like placing it in the old "low-yield corral." If you want to color your retirement green, then think about ways to best put your lazy money to work for you. If you have 10 or more years until you need your funds, your options are many and varied. Talk to a competent financial professional who specializes in retirement income planning and take note of just how many strategies are open to you. Often, a review will cost you absolutely nothing but could result in your obtaining a new consciousness horizon when it comes to putting your money to work for you in the most efficient manner during your retirement years.

4 Create Your Own Paycheck

It used to be that American workers could put in their 30 or 35 years of service and retire with a pension that would guarantee them a lifetime of income. That, plus their Social Security, would put them in a position where retirement would be comfortably funded. However, pensions started dying out in the 1990s, and it is rare for companies to offer them today. Solution? Create your own paycheck.

Your 401(k) is not a ready-made paycheck. Paychecks should be consistent and predictable. Remember, pensions are defined **benefit** plans that guarantee a certain income, as opposed to the 401(k)'s function as a defined *contribution* program, meaning the only certainty is knowing how much goes ins. With a 401(k), the growth of your retirement account is typically predicated on the performance of mutual funds. If the market continues gaining in value, then so does your retirement account. But if they slide, or, as they did in the decade of the 2000s, remain flat, then your retirement account performs accordingly. I would advise anyone who is receiving a company match into their 401(k) to take it and make the most of it. If your employer is willing to match the amount you put into the program, contribute as much as you possibly can. Usually, there is a maximum you can contribute. Contribute the maximum. It's free money.

If your employer does not provide matching funds, then you have some decision-making to do about whether your 401(k) is the best place to be saving for retirement. Your best option may be a Roth IRA. Roth IRAs provide no tax-deferred contributions, but growth within a Roth IRA is not taxed, and withdrawals are tax-free. There are rules as to whether and when you can roll over from an employer-sponsored 401(k) to a self-directed IRA, so check with financial professionals and with the personnel department where you work.

A self-directed IRA or a fixed index annuity can be one pathway to creating your own paycheck. Modern annuities allow for returns that reflect a portion of the ups of the market with none of the downs. Some of them even offer lifetime income options, the kind that are rapidly gaining in popularity among baby boomers who missed out on pensions.

There are many advantages to having your own personal plan for a paycheck as opposed to having one that a sponsoring company controls. For one thing, you are in charge of it. You make the calls. The younger you are, the more time you have to ensure a healthy monthly payout for the rest of your life. The closer you are to retirement, the more you will need to look at special strategies that a good retirement income specialist can guide you through. Either way, it's never too late to start. One upside to having your own income plan is that you don't have to depend on anyone else but yourself. You are not at the mercies of some big company that can jerk the rug out from under you with a notice posted on the bulletin board or an impersonal letter received from the personnel office. If you are still in your working years and you don't like the environment in which you work, you can pick up stakes and depart for greener pastures without worrying about your income in retirement. You simply take it with you. It's yours. You make the rules.

#5 Live Long and Prosper

"Live long and prosper" was a Vulcan greeting made popular by the late Leonard Nimoy, who played the character of Mister Spock in Star Trek, a science fiction television series that achieved record-breaking popularity in the late 1960s. The show was in color, which was new and exciting in those days. The technology of color television was not as advanced as it is today. My father would spend a considerable amount of time adjusting the color on the television "set," as the TV was called in those days, and woe be unto any who touched those knobs other than him.

Star Trek was one of the best shows to use when adjusting the tuner for just the right color reception. This was because of the vibrant pastel colors of the costumes worn by Captain Kirk and crew as each week they boldly went "where no man had gone before." Burned into my brain is the visual image of the droll Mister Spock holding up his hand in that unusual way, making a "V" out of the four fingers of his right hand, and uttering melodramatically, "Live long and prosper."

I wouldn't know until years later, watching an interview conducted with the actor, that the greeting was not originally part of the Star Trek script. Nimoy said he just came up with the idea on the set one day to make a scene more believable. His pointy-eared character was supposed to be returning to his home planet for some Vulcan ceremony and Nimoy said he just felt like it would be more authentic if the Vulcans had a unique greeting of some kind. He said he remembered a similar Jewish greeting from his childhood and improvised a version of it for the scene.

It stuck, and became so popular that the script writers began putting it nearly every episode.

But to "live long and prosper" is what I wish for you, dear reader, as you boldly go where you have not been before, into what I hope is the most exciting and rewarding time of your life. May the "green" on your set be vibrant and clear, so to speak.

Physical Fitness

As we grow older, we can enjoy life so much more if we exercise and stay as healthy as possible. I don't mean to preach here, but anyone who knows me knows how passionate I am about physical fitness. I have found that as I grow older, I have to discipline myself more and more when it comes to getting what I consider to be the proper amount of exercise every day. And, truthfully, some days I don't. But if we want to enjoy our "golden years," it is vital that we give attention to this side of life.

I have read that once you pass the age of 25, your total body strength decreases by 4 percent every decade. But regular physical exercise can help combat the loss of muscle strength and bring back that flexibility and endurance.

Babs and I love to walk. But pulling ourselves away from some project in which we have become engrossed, or setting aside obligations for just that 30 to 45 minutes is sometimes difficult. After the walk is underway, however, I am reminded of how important it is to "stop and smell the roses" at regular intervals in our lives.

According to statistics, the baby boom generation is scheduled to live longer than any generation before it. Who would have thought it? This is the generation that once subscribed to the motto coined by Jerry Rubin and made popular by Bob Dylan, "*never trust anyone over 30.*" And which band was it that sang, "hope I die before I get old," The Who? Somewhere along the line, they changed their tune, didn't they?

The prospect of living longer is not just unbridled optimism on boomers' part. Even insurance actuaries and federal budget projections predict that boomers will live significantly longer than did their parents and grandparents before them. This phenomenon is partly due to better health care and medical advances. But there is a counterbalance to all of this. With every blessing comes a curse, it seems. Boomers are plagued, on average, with elevated rates of obesity, cancer and diabetes. This may be too much of the "good life" taking its toll. Suicide is up for our generation, too. All of this could slow down the longevity, or even reverse it if we're not careful. What you do each day while in your early retirement years forms the matrix for how you will spend your later retirement years.

Define Your Own Retirement

RETIREMENT: the phase in one's life where the balance shifts from work, career and raising a family towards enjoying leisure and personal interests.

That's one definition. The word itself, I think, is a misnomer. To "retire" means, according to the dictionary, to "withdraw, to back away from." I prefer to think of it as a period of advancement toward something. Finally, now that we have our obligations cared for, we can pursue a passion for which, until now, we had limited time to pursue. It could be anything from sailing to playing the piano. We can discover new worlds, heretofore uncharted. We can, as Mister Spock so eloquently put it, "boldly go" where we had never gone before.

May you live long, my friend, and prosper.

ABOUT THE AUTHOR

Jack Teboda has been in the financial services business since 1978. He earned a Bachelor of Science degree from Iowa State University in 1972 and a master's degree from Northern Illinois University in 1974. He has passed the Series 6, 7, 22, 62, 63 and 65 securities exams and holds life, accident and health insurance licenses.

Over the past 37 years, he has gained the knowledge and experience to help others attain financial independence through personalized investment strategies. Jack has also completed the education to earn the designation of Certified Estate Planner (CEP). This continuous education demonstrates the enthusiasm Jack has for his profession, his eagerness to stay current with today's fast-changing financial environment, and his dedication to providing excellent service to his clients.

As a registered Investment Adviser Representative with AE Wealth Management, LLC, Jack is able to offer a wide variety of financial options and products to fit the needs of his clients.

Jack grew up in DeKalb, Illinois, and now resides in Elgin, Illinois, with his wife of more than 40 years, Babs. They have three children: Blakely of Minnesota, Kylee of Illinois and Trace of Colorado, as well as two grandchildren. He is an avid golfer and is actively involved with the Harvest Bible Chapel of Elgin.

ACKNOWLEDGEMENTS

A project such as this just does not happen without the support of many people who gave selflessly of their time, wisdom and energy to bring it about. I would like to thank my wife, Babs, whose patience with me knows no bounds. I apologize for the blank stares you sometimes received when we were talking and my mind was off somewhere in the pages of this book. I promise to make it up to you.

I could never have finished by deadline without the able assistance of my administrative team at Teboda & Associates. Christina Strissel and Zackery Fall were kind enough to help me with some of the research that went into this project and for their able assistance, I will be forever grateful.

No effort so concentrated and intense as writing a book could be carried out without the support of my talented and skilled colleagues, Kevin Sanders and Amanda Jager.

I have been fortunate indeed to have the able assistance of Sheila Burnette, who helped me proof-read the galleys of this publication, and Sharon Coker, who guided this project with vision and helped immeasurably in steering the overall tone of the book.

Conversations throughout the past three decades of my professional life have helped forge the direction this book has taken. I offer my sincere gratitude to the following individuals whose ardent search for truth in wealth management strategies and techniques have mirrored my own: Lee Hyder, Bob Harwood, Bob Fugate, Chris Hobart and Isaac Wright. I especially appreciate the humor and wit of my good friend

Mike Reese, whose patience and forbearance simply cannot be over-looked.

I have been fortunate to be associated with Advisors Excel for many years now, and their talent and energy never ceases to amaze me. My thanks to the founders: Derek Thompson, Cody Foster and David Callanan; as well as Matt Neuman and his entire team. I would also like to thank my copy editor, Tom Bowen, for his talent and expertise; as well as Mallory McDaniel and the entire creative department at Advisors Excel for their invaluable assistance in getting this information into printed form. And I cannot forget the contributions of Mike Meek, Gina Rainey and Joel Johnson, both personally and professionally.

Most importantly, I want to thank my Lord and savior, who has blessed me with the gift of being able to help people work toward financial independence, something which continues to give me immeasurable satisfaction in life. He has also surrounded me with extraordinary people in my workplace, which makes my job a true joy every day. Through him, all things are possible and we must never forget to thank him each day for the countless blessings he bestows on each and every one of us.

www.ingramcontent.com/pod-product-compliance
Lightning Source LLC
Chambersburg PA
CBHW071447180526
45170CB00001B/497